F-18 HORI

HERMAN J. SIXMA &
THEO W. VAN GEFFEN

IAN ALLAN
Publishing

First published 1993

ISBN 0 7110 1944 4

Published by Ian Allan Ltd,
Shepperton, Surrey; and printed
in Great Britain by
Ian Allan Printing Ltd,
Coombelands House,
Addlestone, Surrey KT15 1HY

Front cover:
**F/A-18A (161926, -305) VFA-
113 USS *Constellation*.**
McDonnell Douglas

Back cover:
An unidentified F/A-18.
Theo W. Van Geffen, IAAP

Title Page:
***F/A-18A (161744, EC-11)
YMFA-531 MCAS El Toro, Ca.
A 'Grey Ghost' armed with
500lb bombs ready for a dawn
MABEX support mission.***
Frank Mormillo

PREFACE

From a photographer's point of view, the trouble with the colour
schemes of today's US Marine Corps and Navy aircraft is that they
make for boring photographs. We look back with nostalgia to the
period when the aircraft still carried bright and brilliant colour
schemes. This has been particularly the case during the compilation
of this album. At least when we covered the F-14 Tomcat, we could
include photographs of the pre-grey and dull low-viz colour
schemes. With the Hornet we could not, simply because it was not
even flying operationally at that time.

To 'relieve the pain' a little bit, some (Navy) squadron
commanders take the chance to paint a maximum of two of their
aircraft in the traditional colourful squadron markings. And,
fortunately enough, the RAAF (Royal Australian Air Force) flies its
F/A-18 Hornets with traditional bright and brilliant squadron
markings. In addition to Australia, Canada and Spain fly the Hornet
as well (with Kuwait and Switzerland to follow), making this album
not merely a compilation of Marine Corps and Navy F/A-18s.

It was tough, but fun to compile this book. We'd like to thank the
following: Lt Lydia Zeller, Lt Fred Henney (both Chinfo), LCdr Gene
Okamoto (NAS Point Mugu), Dennis McGrath (NAS Lemoore), Cdr
Dottie Schmidt (USNR), Chief Randy Gaddo, Capt Linda Western
(both USMC), the PAO Shop at MCAS Beaufort, Ken Carter (DDI),
Russell Egnor (Chinfo), Capt Yves Généreux and Mr Lusignan (CAF),
Greg Meggs, Peter Foster, AIR (Don Spering), Frank Mormillo, Keith
Snyder and last but not least Tom Downey and Daryl Stephenson
(McDonnell Douglas).

Theo W. van Geffen (IAAP)
Herman J. Sixma (IAAP)
Utrecht, Holland

The Hornet Story

When VFA-125, the first F/A-18 squadron in the US Navy, took delivery of its premier Hornet on 19 February 1981, a new milestone had been reached on a long and difficult road towards a new type of aircraft for the US Navy. Long, because the history of the McDonnell Douglas F/A-18 Hornet can be traced back to the Northrop P-530 Cobra, designed in the late 1960s. Difficult, because during the development and test programme, not only were serious doubts raised about its original basic design as a Light Weight Fighter (LWF), but also about the ability of one man to cope with the workload of a dual-role aircraft.

At the same time the US Air Force was also involved in selecting a new Air Combat Fighter (ACF). After its test programme and a formal evaluation at the end of 1974, it was announced on 13 January 1975 that the USAF had selected the General Dynamics YF-16 over the Northrop YF-17, although the latter type had certainly proven to be superior in several aspects. The US Navy was looking for an aircraft to replace its ageing F-4 Phantoms and A-7 Corsairs, as well as to supplement the F-14 which had become too expensive to acquire in the number originally specified. Solutions like a cheaper F-14, a navalised F-15 and improved F-4, were rejected by the Navy in favour of a new Naval Air Combat Fighter (NACF) with a secondary attack capability, designated VFAX (Fighter/Attack Experimental Aeroplane). As a result of a decision by Congress, the VFAX contest was cancelled in favour of a competition between the derivatives of the Air Force ACF contest. The prize in this NACF contest would be an order for some 800 fighter aircraft.

The two manufacturers involved in the ACF contest teamed up with other companies that could offer extensive backgrounds in the design and construction of naval aircraft: General Dynamics with Ling-Temco-Vought, and Northrop with McDonnell Douglas. The GD/LTV combination entered the competition with Models 1600, 1601 and 1602. The Northrop/McDonnell Douglas proposal, designated McDonnell Douglas Model 267, was a combination of Northrop's YF-17 navalised version, called P-630, and the first fruits of McDonnell Douglas' involvement in the NACF contest. After a series of modifications the Navy announced, on 2 May 1975, that Model 267 met the requirements best. The choice was controversial, however: the aircraft was the loser in the ACF competition and not, as Congress had supposedly proclaimed to the Navy, a version of the winner. The Navy commented that it had simply selected the aircraft most suitable to fit its needs. The prime contractor for the now called F-18 was McDonnell Douglas, with Northrop as the principal subcontractor. The construction work was split approximately 60:40. McDonnell Douglas was responsible for the forward fuselage, wings, horizontal stabiliser, landing gear, arresting hook and cockpit; and Northrop for the main structural section of the airframe including the centre and aft fuselage, and vertical fins. This workshare was to be reversed in the case of any orders being placed for a land-based version (the F-18L), to be developed by Northrop. (Iran indicated in 1976 that it was interested in buying 250 F-18Ls. This order, however, did not proceed.)

The Navy formed a team of fleet aviation and test pilots, called the Aircrew Systems Advisory Panel to evaluate systems and to provide advice to the contractors. Focuses of attention included the cockpit and the overall design of the weapon systems. One result of the Advisory Panel's attention was the addition of HOTAS (Hands-On-Throttle-And-Stick). On 21 November 1975 General Electric received a contract for the Full Scale Development (FSD) of the F404 engine, a modified YJ101 engine as used in the YF-17.

On 22 January 1976, the US Navy awarded a contract to McDonnell Douglas Corporation for FSD of the F-18. The contract also included a batch of 11 pre-production aircraft, nine single-seaters and two tandem-seaters. A first flight was scheduled to take place in July 1978. The option included 185 aircraft for the Navy and 270 for the Marine Corps in the fighter role (F-18) and 245 aircraft for the Navy in the attack configuration (A-18).

Although the name 'Hornet' had enjoyed fairly widespread use for the Navy ships of the line, Secretary of the Navy W. Graham Claytor

Left:
F/A-18C (163765, 'NH-305') 'VFA-22', NAS Lemoore, Ca
Question: What do you do when you hold an official ceremony to mark the redesignation of your squadron from 'attack squadron' to 'strike fighter squadron', and you still have no aircraft of your own? Answer: You borrow an F/A-18 from a sister squadron (VFA-113, NK-305) and with the use of paint, brushes and cardboard, paint it in your own squadron markings and then cover the original markings of the borrowed Hornet with your new ones!

This actually took place on 3 May 1990, one day before VA-22 was to be officially redesignated VFA-22, marking the end of a long period of A-7 Corsair II flying. The last A-7E was lost on 26 April 1990.

VFA-22 is still part of CVW-11. The Air Wing was last aboard USS _Enterprise_ (CVN-65), but was assigned to the new USS _Abraham Lincoln_ (CVN-72), after _Lincoln's_ transfer to NAS Alameda, Ca, and _Enterprise's_ two-year recess for a comprehensive overhaul.
Theo W. van Geffen, IAAP

Above left:

F/A-18A (163158, VM-13) VMFA-451, MCAS Beaufort, SC
The Marine Corps Air Station (MCAS) at Beaufort, South Carolina,
houses six Marine Fighter Attack Squadrons (VMFA), which are
equipped with the A-version of the F/A-18 Hornet. Plans for what
has become the present installation were in the development
stages as far back as the summer of 1941. The airport was
commissioned Naval Air Station, Beaufort, on 15 June 1943.

One of the squadrons assigned to the present air station is
VMFA-451 'Warlords'. The original 'Warlords' were activated at
MCAS Mojave, Ca, 15 February 1944, flying F-4U Corsairs.

After a period of inactivation (10 September 1945-1 July 1946),
VMFA-451 was reactivated as part of the Marine Air Reserve
Training Command at NAS Willow Grove, Pa. With the outbreak of
the Korean War, the squadron was called to active duty on 1 March
1951. On 1 July 1961 the 'Warlords' were redesignated as Marine
All Weather Fighter Squadron — (VMF(AW)-451 — and assigned 18
F-8U Crusaders. During the following January VMF(AW)-451
completed the first transpacific flight by a single-seat aircraft,
when the squadron deployed to NAS Atsugi, Japan. A new
redesignation followed on 1 February 1968 when the F-8s were

traded in for F-4J Phantoms and the unit became VMFA-451. The
first 'S' version of the F-4 arrived in June 1978. After departure to
AMARC of the last two F-4S aircraft on 26 October 1986,
conversion to the F/A-18 started, the squadron becoming
operational as a Hornet unit in July 1987. F/A-18 No 500 (163133)
was delivered to VMFA-451 on 15 May 1987 and received 'VM-02'
markings.

The 'Warlords' were part of CVW-13 aboard USS *Coral Sea*
(tailcode AK) during a 6th Fleet cruise from 31 May-30 September,
1989. VMFA-451 won the CY-90 CNO Aviation Safety Award 'S',
winning the award for the third consecutive year. In early 1990 the
squadron had flown 45,900hr without a major mishap, completing
12 years of accident-free flying. *Theo van Geffen, IAAP*

Above:

F/A-18A (163132, VM-01) VMFA-451, MCAS Beaufort, SC
Flying in the company of a RAF Tornado F3 over the Saudi desert,
this VMFA-451 F/A-18A is equipped for CAP (Combat Air Patrol)
with two AIM-9L Sidewinders and two AIM-7F Sparrows.
Sqn Ldr T. Paxton

announced on 1 March 1977 that the F-18 would be called the 'Hornet'. In December 1977 Navy test pilots based at NAS Point Mugu, Ca, tested and evaluated the YF-17 in a series of flights. Flying qualities and performance characteristics were commented upon favourably, providing a basis for confidence that the production F-18 aircraft would perform in a similar fashion.

On 17 March 1978 forward and aft sections of the first Hornet (160775) were mated at Northrop's Hawthorne facility, almost six months later followed by the roll-out of the aircraft at St Louis, Mo (13 September 1978). The first flight of the F-18 took place on 18 November 1978 with Chief Test Pilot Jack Krings at the controls. On 16 January 1979 the Hornet arrived at NAS Patuxent River, Md, to continue contractor's testing and for evaluation trials by the Naval Air Test Center (NATC). In fact, the F-18 Hornet was the first type of aircraft for the US Navy of which almost all flight-testing took place from NAS Patuxent River. This single-site testing concept allowed personnel from the Navy and McDonnell Douglas to work closely together and to ensure early implementation of any Navy comments on design. It would also enable the Navy to make hands-on assessments of the aircraft during preliminary evaluations leading up to BIS (Board of Inspection and Survey) service acceptance trials. Previous test programmes were all carried out on a variety of locations. The full-scale development testing took place through October 1982, totalling more than 3,000 test flights and 6,000 flying hours. To support F-18 test operations the NATC received additional Skywarrior tanker, Skyhawk target and Phantom chase aircraft. A North American Rockwell T-39D Sabreliner (150987) was modified to serve as a flying test-bed for the F-18's radar. Aboard the Sabreliner were the Hornet's Hughes APG-65 radar, mission computer, displays and INS (Inertial Navigation Systems), which form the core of the Hornet's airborne electronics or avionics ability. A preliminary evaluation of the radar and avionics integration was completed in July 1979. The integration received 70hr of testing aboard the T-39.

The programme also involved a number of carrier suitability trials. After a series of 70 catapult launches and 120 arrester-gear landings at Patuxent River, carrier suitability trials were carried out by the third Hornet (160777) from USS America (CV-66) in the period 30 October-3 November 1979. During the four days, 32 catapult launches and traps were made together with 17 bolters (touch-and-go landings). The first missile — a heat-seeking Sidewinder — was launched from an F-18 on 26 December 1979. The target was a radio-controlled BQM-34 drone. TF-18A No 1 (160781), the first two-seat version, arrived at NATC in December 1979, after a first flight on 25 October 1979. The TF-18 remained fully combat capable. Less than 6% of the single-place Hornet's internal fuel capacity is sacrificed for the second cockpit. A second batch of sea trials, including a series of fully automatic hands-off landings, was made in August 1982 aboard USS Carl Vinson (CVN-70) and involved 63 catapult launches and arrester-gear landings.

During the flight tests two serious accidents occurred. On 8 September 1980, Hornet T2 (160784) crashed near RAF Middle Wallop in England due to problems with the left engine. Both pilots ejected safely. Two months later, on 14 November 1980, a production aircraft (161215) crashed into Chesapeake Bay, after the pilot had lost control at about 20,000ft and ejected safely. Following this accident a spin recovery switch was incorporated to the flight computer control of all production Hornets.

The Defense Systems Acquisition Review Council (DSARC) had recommended on 8 December 1982 that the Hornet be approved for full production in the bomber role. To stress this dual role of the Hornet, the new designation became F/A-18; F/A-18A for the single-seater and F/A-18B for the two-seater. The fighter configuration had been given the Council's approval in June 1981, after which the Secretary of Defense approved full production of the Hornet on 29 June. A total of 1,157 F/A-18 Hornets have been ordered by the US Navy and Marine Corps to support both air-to-air and air-to-ground attack missions. Of this number the AO (Acquisition Objective) for the Marine Corps is 500 and for the Navy 657 aircraft. An amendment to the FY92/93 defense budget contained a request to raise this number because of inflationary reasons (for FY92 + 12 and FY93 + 28). Although the F/A-18 production was to be terminated after the FY93 lot, a supplemental request for 54 F/A-18s each in FY94/96 was approved, after which the F/A-18E/F is scheduled for production. The F/A-18 reached IOC (Initial Operational Capability) on 7 January 1983, with Marine Fighter Attack Squadron (VMFA)-314 at MCAS El Toro, Ca.

The F/A-18 Hornet in foreign service

Initially, the F/A-18 Hornet had entered service with three foreign air arms. The first country to select the Hornet was Canada. After a detailed evaluation study which started in the autumn of 1977, the competition was narrowed from six types to two: the General Dynamics F-16 and the F-18. A final decision in favour of the Hornet was announced on 10 April 1980. The contract, which was signed six days later called for 113 CF-18As and 25 CF-18B trainers to be built in St Louis, Mo. After a maiden flight on 29 July 1982, the first two production aircraft for the Canadian Armed Forces (CF-18Bs) were delivered to No 410 Operational Training Squadron at CFB Cold Lake, Alberta, on 25 October 1982. The last CF-18A was ferried to Cold Lake on 28 September 1988. All aircraft were delivered to No 410 Squadron for acceptance testing prior to allocation to other squadrons. Differences between the Canadian and US F/A-18s include the Instrument Landing System (ILS), and the addition of a 600,000 candle-power spotlight in the starboard nose section for visual identification during night interceptions. Two squadrons of CF-18s are assigned to NATO; a third squadron — No 409 — was disbanded on 25 June 1991 as part of a plan to reduce personnel stationed at Canadian Forces Europe. CF-18 aircraft and pilots from 409s were reassigned to Nos 421 and 439 Squadrons); four squadrons carry out air defence missions under command of the North American Air Defence (NORAD) and one squadron is the conversion unit; four carry out air defence duties under the command of the North American Air Defence (NORAD), and one squadron is the conversion unit.

Together with the Royal Australian Air Force, at the time of writing, the Canadians are looking at a CF-18 fatigue life management programme. Structural modifications are considered in the mid-1990s to extend the life of the CF-18 airframe into the 21st century. Although originally it was thought that the airframe would have a lifespan of 20 years, the extensive low-level performance of the CF-18 has reduced the lifetime expectation to 10-12 years.

The second country which selected the F/A-18 Hornet was Australia. The order for a total of 75 aircraft — 57 As and 18 Bs — was signed on 20 October 1981, with the first two to be manufactured by McDonnell Douglas. The remainder was to be built under license by Aero Space Technologies of Australia (ASTA) at their Avalon facility, at first from acquired MCAIR parts and later from indigenously manufactured parts. The two McDonnell Douglas-assembled aircraft were flown to RAAF Williamtown, NSW, on 17 May 1985. The first aircraft which was assembled in Australia made its maiden flight on 26 February 1985 and was subsequently assigned to No 2 Operational Conversion Unit (OCU) on 4 May 1985. The first 'all-Australian' Hornet took the air on 3 June 1985. On 16 May 1990, the 75th and last F/A-18 Hornet (A21-57) was accepted during a ceremony at Fairbairn Air Base. The year 1990

was also the beginning of a comprehensive, fleet-wide F/A-18 commonality upgrade by ASTA which will last about two years. The Australians are also interested in bringing their F/A-18As and Bs to the C and D standard. At the time of writing, the Australian Hornets equip three operational squadrons and one conversion unit.

The third export customer for the F/A-18 Hornet is Spain. In May 1983, the Spanish Government announced its plans to order 72 EF-18s (the suffix 'E' stands for *España*). It consisted of 60 single-seat and 12 dual-seat aircraft. The first Hornet, an EF-18B, was formally accepted by the Spanish Air Force at St Louis on 22 November 1985 and made its first flight on 4 December 1985. It was flown — together with three others — to Spain on 10 July 1986. The final two EF-18As were delivered to the Spanish Air Force on 31 July 1990. In Spain the A model is designated C15, the C standing for *Caza* (fighter) and the B, CF15 for *Caza de Entrenamiento* (fighter trainer). The aircraft are assigned to four *Escuadrones* (Squadrons).

The delivery of 40 F/A-18 Hornets to the Kuwaiti Air Force will take place through a FMS (Foreign Military Sales) deal. No instructions were given to stop the production after Iraq's seizure of Kuwait in 1990. At that time the aircraft were in the early stages of production. The first of 40 Kuwaiti Hornets, F/A-18D 441, rolled out at St Louis on 8 October 1991. Powered by the new F-404-GE-402 Enhanced Performance Engines.

On 3 October 1988, it was announced that a proposal to procure 34 Hornets would be submitted to the Swiss Parliament. The F/A-18 was selected in the final stages against the F-16 to fulfil Switzerland's next generation high-level interceptor requirement. In the evaluation process the Canadian Armed Forces leased a CF-18B to McDonnell Douglas (188926) in No 410 Squadron markings) which arrived in Switzerland on 31 March 1988. The contract was scheduled to be signed in September/October 1990. However, due to the changes in the European political situation, and to allow time to examine a national defence review on the 1990s, the signing of the contract was postponed. Also, in this respect, the Swiss Air Force was told to re-evaluate the Mirage 2000-5, which was offered (again), this time at 'a very interesting' price. The outcome of the examination was announced on 26 June 1991 by the Swiss Federal Military Department: 'The F/A-18 meets our military requirements to the fullest extent'. In all two finished aircraft and kits for 32 additional aircraft plus spares, technical support and training are included in the programme involving 26Cs and 8Ds.

The Republic of Korea was to have become a customer for the

A third country to prefer the F/A-18 to the F-16 Fighting Falcon was Spain making it the first Hornet customer in Europe. Although the Spanish Air Force had 144 Hornets on its wish-slip, budgetary constraints reduced the number to 72. The 72 EF-18s would replace the ageing Mirage III, the SF-5 Freedom Fighter and the F-4C Phantom aircraft in the Spanish inventory. The contract was signed on 31 May 1983, and included 60 EF-18As and 12 EF-18Bs. Some 36 aircraft would be delivered in 1986, 24 in 1987 and 12 in 1988. But because of financial difficulties, deliveries also took place in 1989 and 1990. (Eleven Hornets arrived in Spain in 1986, 26 in 1987, 15 in 1988, 12 in 1989 and eight in 1990.)

After completion of the training by McDonnell Douglas of 10 Spanish Air Force instructors, four EF-18Bs made a nonstop flight to Zaragoza on 10 July 1986. The final Spanish Hornet was delivered on 31 July 1990.

Fighter Wing 15 (*Ala de Caza 15*) was the first wing to be equipped with the EF-18. It was established at Zaragoza on 16 December 1985, but had to wait until 10 July 1986 to receive its first aircraft. The Wing's components, Nos 151 and 152 Squadrons (*Escuadrones*), each have 15 single-seaters and three two-seaters. IOC was achieved on 1 November 1988. The second Hornet wing is Fighter Wing 12, which shared Torrejon Air Base with USAFE's 401st Tactical Fighter Wing. Before converting to the EF-18, the Wing had operated the F-4C Phantom. Nos 121 and 122 Squadrons are assigned to Fighter Wing 12. The Wing still has a squadron of RF-4Cs assigned (No 124 Squadron).

Far left:
F/A-18D (441) Kuwaiti Air Force
Hornet 1044 the first in a batch of 40 F/A-18s for the Kuwaiti Air Force on the day of its roll-out on 8 October 1991. *McDonnell Douglas*

Left:
EF-18B (151-02, CE15-2) Ala 15, Zaragoza Air Base (Spain)
The second EF-18 Hornet for the Spanish Air Force, seen here in its element in the skies of Missouri. The aircraft carries the code '151-02' on the nose, denoting it will be assigned to No 151 Squadron after arrival in Spain. In 1987 the three-digit squadron code was changed to the two-wing code. *McDonnell Douglas*

Hornet as well. On 20 December 1989 it was announced that the RoKAF had selected the F/A-18 Hornet to fulfil the Korean Fighter Programme through the acquisition of 120 aircraft, the first of which would be delivered around October 1993. However, a price increase for the F/A-18s beyond the allocated budget range and a reduction in the defence budget necessitated the cancellation of the F/A-18 purchase plans. Instead a number of 120 Block 50 F-16C/D Fighting Falcons will be acquired, saving South Korea around US $1 billion.

Last July McDonnell Douglas submitted a proposal to the US Navy to sell 67 F/A-18s to Finland under a FMS (Foreign Military Sale) agreement. Technically, the US Navy will be the seller. The Finnish Air Force is looking at a follow-on aircraft for its MiG-21bis and SAAB J-35 Draken. Other aircraft in the competition are the SAAB JAS-39 Gripen, General Dynamics F-16 and Dassault Mirage 2000-5.

Finally, the IDF (Israeli Defence Force) expressed an interest in the F/A-18 Hornet, although no formal request has been received yet.

A possible contender to acquire 20 second-hand (RAAF) Hornets was the French Aéronavale. *Was*, because the French Government decided not to purchase the F/A-18 as an interim replacement for its 23 Vought F-8E (FN) Crusaders until the navalised version of the Dassault Rafale D becomes operational, but to retain its Crusaders.

From F/A-18A/B to F/A-18E/F

Deliveries of the F/A-18 Hornet to the US Navy and Marine Corps will continue in the years to come, with the improved and updated single-seat F/A-18C being the current (1991) production standard aircraft. The most important capability improvement consists of the ability to carry the AIM-120 AMRAAM (Advanced Medium-Range Air-to-Air Missile) and the infra red imaging AGM-65F Maverick air-to-surface missile. The first F/A-18C (163427) made its maiden flight on 3 September 1986 and was subsequently delivered to NATC at NAS Patuxent River on 23 September. On 22 October 1986 the first F/A-18D two-seater (163434), which is currently the production standard two-seater, made its first flight and was flown to Patuxent River. Since October 1989, all single-seat 'C' and two-seat 'D' Hornets delivered to the US Navy and Marine Corps are equipped with additional night attack systems and sensors. After the approval of the Night Attack Program in December 1984, the night attack avionics were flight-tested in early 1988 aboard prototype F/A-18D 163434. Its first fully equipped night attack test hop was made on

6 May 1988. After initial flight-testing, the aircraft was flown to NAS China Lake, Ca (Naval Weapons Center) for a seven-month test programme.

The first production night attack F/A-18C (163985) arrived at Patuxent River on 1 November 1989, while the first F/A-18D (163986) followed on 14 November. The night attack version is equipped with a new forward-looking infra red (FLIR) sensor made by Hughes Aircraft Co and called Thermal Imaging Navigation Set (TINS), designed to help pilots navigate and assist in locating, identifying and attacking ground targets at night. Two other important features include Night Vision Goggles (NVG) attached to the pilot's helmet and a colour digital moving map, displaying navigational data and vital intelligence information. Data for the map is stored on a laser disk. Within the US Marine Corps, the F/A-18D two-seater is used as a tactical aircraft, while the US Navy continues to use the F/A-18D in the traditional training role. The new night attack F/A-18Cs and Ds which are currently being delivered to the US Navy and US Marines, will continue to serve into the 21st century.

Future C and D models of the F/A-18 will have provision for the AN/ALQ-165 Airborne Self Protecting Jammer (ASPJ). When fully integrated, the ASPJ will counter the threat posed by the latest radars and missiles. They will also have enhanced engines, the EPE (Enhanced Performance Engine), which is a derivative of the F404-GE-400 engine. EPE-equipped Hornet deliveries begun in 1992. Other upgrades currently planned for the F/A-18C/D include mission computer improvements, reconnaissance capability and development of a lightweight internal cannon to replace the current M61-A1 20mm Gatling gun. The most significant upgrade, however, will be the one to the APG-65 radar, leading to the (Hughes) APG-73. A production contract was signed in June 1991 estimated at $257 million. The agreement covers the production readiness and actual production of 12 radars in the third block of FY92 F/A-18 procurement. The Canadian Forces are also participating as part of a NATO co-operative development programme. This upgrade will increase the speed and memory of the radar's signal and data processors by more than three times. Production deliveries of the APG-73 equipped F/A-18s begin in June 1994.

McDonnell Douglas is even looking further ahead and is working on an updated version of the Hornet: the F/A-18E and F/A-18F. The E and F versions grew out of a study requested by former Secretary of Defense Caspar Weinberger. Beginning in 1987 it was conducted by the Naval Air Systems Command (NAVAIR), McDonnell Douglas

Some 1½ years after Canada's selection of the F/A-18 Hornet, Australia followed, becoming McDonnell Douglas' second export customer in October 1981. The aircraft that would be replaced, after 21 years of service, was the Dassault Mirage III O/OD. As in the case of Canada, an extensive evaluation of several types took place, resulting in the selection of the Hornet. The Royal Australian Air Force (RAAF) also concluded that the Hornet's twin-engines, the excellent attrition and maintenance rates, the advanced avionics and superior performance could not be beaten by any other type in its class. Yet there was a difference: the Australians decided to licence-build the majority of the F/A-18s. The first two RAAF Hornets were manufactured in St Louis, while the initial batch of production aircraft was assembled from imported parts by Aero Space Technologies of Australia in Avalon. Australia would also build most of the F404-GE-400 engines.

As compared to the US Marine Corps/US Navy F/A-18A, the Australian Hornet has no catapult launch equipment, but it does have a High Frequency (HF) radio for long-range communications and a conventional ILS.

The two F/A-18Bs that were built by McDonnell Douglas (A21-101/102) were handed over to the RAAF on 29 October 1984. During the 15hr ferry flight to Australia, the Hornets were accompanied by USAF KC-10s and were then assigned to No 2 OCU (Operational Conversion Unit) at RAAF Williamtown, NSW, on 17 May 1985. Due to the introduction of the F/A-18, and in order to accommodate two operational squadrons and the OCU, RAAF Williamtown was extensively modernised at a cost of more than A$100 million. To control the Hornet squadrons at RAAF Williamtown, the 81st Fighter Wing was activated on 2 February 1987. The RAAF suffered its first F/A-18 casualty on 18 November 1987, when F/A-18B A21-104 crashed 40 miles Northwest of Townsville, Queensland. Double the amount of money spent at RAAF Williamtown had to be spent to refurbish RAAF Tindal, Northern Territories (NT). The base had to be rebuilt almost completely in order to house the RAAF's fourth F/A-18 unit.

Instead of the permanent Mirage presence in Malaysia, detachments to Singapore and Butterworth totalling some 16 weeks are made twice a year, the first detachment taking place in September 1988.

Below:
F/A-18A (A21-21)   No 75 Squadron, Tindal, NT
The last RAAF squadron to convert to the F/A-18 was No 75 Squadron. Until the arrival of its first Hornet in May 1988, No 75 Squadron had operated the Mirage III O/OD from Darwin, NT. The unit was PCS-ed (Permanent Change of Station) to RAAF Tindal, NT, in September 1988 and achieved IOC status on 1 October 1988.
Greg Meggs

and Northrop. Its objectives were to identify potential enhancements to the F/A-18 that would ensure it could fulfil the Navy's requirements for a versatile, affordable strike fighter into the 21st century. The study defined seven upgrade approaches for the F/A-18, of which the F/A-18E/F represents NAVAIR's preferred configuration. It builds upon several incremental upgrades, already underway for the C/D, and is based also on the improvements identified in the Hornet 2000 study. Both the single seat E and the two-seat F models will have greater range and payload performances, more powerful engines, increased carrier bring-back capabilities, and growth provisions for advanced avionics and weapons systems.

A modification to the F/A-18's airframe is the primary feature of the E/F upgrade. Structural changes include slightly longer fuselage (+ 4.1ft), and an enlarged wing (+ 100sq ft). The changes will increase the aircraft's internal fuel capacity by 3,000lb (extending the Hornet's mission radius up to 40%, depending on mission specifics.) The larger wing improves flight characteristics and includes two additional external weapons stations. Increased engine power (+ 12,000lb thrust) will be provided by F404 derivative engines. Proposed changes to the crew station include an eight-by-eight inch tactical situation display and a touchscreen up-front display. The FY92/93 budget request includes $1.4 billion for the development of the new Hornet versions. Through the extension of the F/A-18 programme the gap can be filled until an alternative for the cancelled A-12A Avenger II has been found. The first F/A-18E should fly in 1995. Initial operating capability (IOC) could be reached in 1998. It is thought that the structure of the Carrier Air Wing of the future will consist by 2010 of 42 F/A-18E/Fs and 18 AXs (replacement for the A-6), while the F-14 will be gone.

Below:

F/A-18B (A21-108)   No 3 Squadron, Williamtown, NSW
No 3 Squadron became the RAAF's first operational Hornet squadron. Before starting conversion in May 1986, No 3 Squadron had operated with 12 Mirage III O aircraft in Butterworth, Malaysia. It disbanded on 31 March 1986, giving the Mirage aircraft to the newly reformed No 79 Squadron at Butterworth, but reformed at RAAF Williamtown, NSW, one day later. Its first F/A-18 was welcomed on 30 August that same year, and arrived from No 2 OCU. The squadron has a multi-role mission, but also has a responsibility of developing F/A-18 air-to-air attacks. *Greg Meggs*

Below:
F/A-18A (A21-25) No 77 Squadron, Williamtown, NSW
RAAF Williamtown's third Hornet unit is No 77 Squadron. It reformed as an F/A-18 unit on 1 July 1987. Before conversion, No 77 Squadron had flown the Mirage III O/OD. After also receiving No 2 OCU's Mirages, No 77 Squadron became the largest RAAF squadron since World War 2 with 43 Mirages and 16 MB326H aircraft assigned. No 77's mission was Mirage pilot conversion,

Mirage fighter combat instructor courses and Macchi introductory fighter courses. In early 1987, No 77 Squadron also received a number of Winjeels to train FACs (Forward Air Controllers). The lead-in training mission and MB326H aircraft were transferred to No 2 OCU after conversion to Hornet. Besides its normal multi-role mission, No 77 Squadron develops air-to-ground tactics.
Greg Meggs

Below left:
F/A-18A (A21-1) No 2 OCU, Williamtown, NSW
No 2 OCU at RAAF Williamtown, NSW, is responsible for the training of RAAF Hornet pilots. To accomplish this mission, the OCU has some 14 aircraft assigned. The squadron had operated as the Mirage training unit and also had been tasked with the lead-in training role in the MB326H. The mission and aircraft were transferred to No 77 Squadron when No 2 OCU stood down in December 1984. The first Hornets were received in May 1985. When No 77 Squadron converted to the F/A-18, No 2 OCU resumed its old mission of lead-in training, consequently receiving back the MB326s. However, mission and aircraft were later transferred to No 76 Squadron, also at RAAF Williamtown. *Greg Meggs*

Canada became the first export customer for the F/A-18 Hornet. The mission of the Canadian Hornet is fulfiling the air defence role within NORAD (North American Air Defence) and the tactical fighter role in support of Canada's NATO obligations in Europe. To accomplish this mission the Canadian Armed Forces possess six CF-18 squadrons, of which four are stationed in Canada (Nos 416, 425, 433 and 441 Squadrons) and responsible to Air Command's Fighter Group. The remaining two in Germany (No 421 and 439 Squadrons) are responsible to Canadian Forces Europe's 4th Fighter Wing (which is assigned to the 1 (Canadian Air Division). In a recent move to reduce personnel stationed at Canadian Forces Europe, the third Canadian Squadron (409) was disbanded on 25 June 1991 with the pilots and aircraft being reassigned to the other two squadrons. In addition, Canada-based No 410 Squadron takes care of the training of new Hornet pilots, while the Aircraft Engineering Test Establishment (AETE) also possesses some CF-18A/B aircraft. Two of the Canada-based fighter squadrons (Nos 416 and 433) are designated Rapid Reinforcement NATO squadrons and will deploy to Lahr (Germany) to reinforce NATO in times of tension, under 3 Fighter Wing.

The Hornet has replaced the CF-101 Voodoo, CF-104 Starfighter and CF-5 Freedom Fighter. One of the main reasons why the Canadians selected the Hornet was the safety aspect of a twin-engined aircraft over Canada's frozen north.

Until January 1984, when the first operational unit started the conversion to the Hornet, time was used to produce the conversion syllabus and to form the nucleus of Hornet instructors. However, the first group of pilots went through training with VFA-125 at NAS Lemoore, Ca. By the end of July 1984, deliveries of CF-18s from St Louis were suspended following the discovery of fatigue cracks in the stub attachments for the central fins. Several aircraft were grounded, while flying was severely restricted pending modifications. The result was a delay and change in the re-equipment programme. In succession, the following squadrons formed or reformed on the CF-18: No 409 'Nighthawk', No 425 'Alouette', No 439 'Tiger', No 421 'Red Indian', No 441 'Silver Fox', No 433 'Porcupine' and No 416 'Black Lynx'.

On 23 April 1990, all CF-18s were grounded for at least 48hr after the fourth accident in the course of that year involving the loss of four pilots and five Hornets. Six other CF-18s had been lost since the aircraft had been operational in 1982. Human error seemed to be the only common thread found in the mishaps, rather than any deficiency in the airframe and/or engines. In late September 1991 the Canadian Department of National Defense announced further reductions in their forces in Europe, which are in line with overall European defense cutbacks. The cuts will include the closure of Baden-Söllingen Air Base by 1994 and Lahr Air Base by 1995, and the withdrawal of both 421 and 439 Squadrons to Canada. The 1st (Canadian) Air Division will be downgraded to an Air Group in 1992. After the return of the two units two CF-18 Hornet Squadrons in Canada will receive the 'as needed' status for deployment to Europe and use by NATO in case of a crisis.

Above right:

CF-18A (188739) 1 CAG, Baden-Söllingen AB, Germany
Until 15 June 1991 the Air Division consisted of three CF-18 units: Nos 409, 421 and 439 Squadrons. Although No 409 Squadron was planned to become the first operational Canada-based unit, the re-equipment programme had to be changed because of fin fatigue problems and a shortage of spares. Consequently the 'Nighthawks' (their motto is 'midnight is our noon') were transferred to Baden-Söllingen and replaced No 441 Squadron. Its first four CF-18s arrived on 30 May 1985. No 421 Squadron disbanded as a CF-104 unit on 1 October 1985 and was reactivated on 22 May 1986 as a CF-18 unit. No 439 Squadron reformed at Baden-Söllingen on 29 November 1985. 1AD was reactivated at Lahr on 28 May 1988, replacing 1CAG.

In this photograph two 1CAG CF-18As touch down at Kleine Brogel's runway after finishing a mission in Tactical Air Meet (TAM) 1986. *Theo van Geffen, IAAP*

Right:

CF-18A (188709) No 410 Squadron, Cold Lake, Alberta
CF-18A (188760) No 421 Squadron, Baden-Söllingen, Germany
A rare combination: a Cold Lake-based No 410 Squadron CF-18A in formation with a Baden-Söllingen-stationed No 421 Squadron CF-18. The 'Red Indians' became the third Canadian unit in Germany to convert to the Hornet (the name 'Hornet' is not officially accepted by the Canadians). Aircraft flown in the past by the squadron were the Spitfire, Sabre and Starfighter. *Peter Foster*

Right:

CF-18As (188728 and others) No 409 Squadron, Baden Söllingen, Germany
A formation of No 409 CF-18As over Southern Germany. *Canadian Forces by WO Vic Johnson*

Below right:

CF-18A (188742) No 409 Squadron, Doha, Qatar
A CF-18A of No 439 Squadron on the taxiway at Doha ready to take-off for CAP. It is equipped with three 330 US gal fuel tanks, two AIM-9 Sidewinder and four AIM-7 Sparrow air-to-air missiles. Note the Arabic on the leading edge root extension. Before 'Desert Storm' started the CF-18s were on QRA; during the operation they flew round-the-clock missions.
Canadian Forces

After the unanimous approval of the United Nations Security Council, Resolution 661 imposed economic sanctions on Iraq on 6 August 1990. Four days later Canada's Prime Minister announced that he would contribute two destroyers and a supply ship to aid a multi-national military effort in the Gulf Region. To provide air cover for the Canadian ships and to augment the multi-national air resources already in place the Prime Minister announced on 14 September 1990 the decision to send a squadron of 18 CF-18s to the Gulf. The entire Canadian effort in the Gulf region would eventually be known as Operation 'Friction'. Qatar agreed to provide an operating base (at Doha) and facilities. The base was nicknamed 'Canada Dry'. Doha was not designed for such a large number of aircraft (USAFE F-16Cs and Qatari and French Mirage F1s were also stationed there). For this reason the CF-18s had to be parked on portable class 60 steel trackways.

Under the Canadian Air Task Group Middle East (CATGME), No 409 (Tactical Fighter) Squadron became the first Canadian unit to deploy to the Gulf on 6 October 1990. Their first CAP was flown one day later. To carry out this mission the CF-18s were equipped with AIM-7 Sparrow and AIM-9 Sidewinder air-to-air missiles in addition to the M-61 20mm cannon. While flying CAP missions, CF-18 pilots received flight control direction through specialised US Navy ships, thus reacting to direction from US controllers, an arrangement which proved very effective.

In mid-December 1990, No 439 (Tactical Fighter) Squadron relieved 409 Squadron. On 11 January 1991 the deployment of six additional CF-18s — from 416 (Tactical Fighter) Squadron, Cold Lake — was announced, while simultaneously a Boeing 707 air-to-air refuelling aircraft was deployed, to enable the Hornets to fly around-the-clock missions, and to assist in refuelling aircraft.

When 'Desert Storm' started on 17 January 1991 the role of the CF-18s was expanded to sweep and escort functions. The sweep mission consisted of air operations dedicated to establishing air superiority over enemy territory. The first two sweep and escort missions with four CF-18s per mission were flown on 21 January, although both missions were called off while the aircraft were in flight because of bad weather. One month later (20 February) the Canadian Minister of National Defence announced that CAF's CF-18s would, once the appropriate equipment was in place, undertake air-to-ground attack missions against military targets inside Kuwait and Iraq, in addition to providing CAPs for allied shipping in the Gulf. While the CF-18s from Baden-Söllingen were deployed to Doha,

Hornets from Canada augmented the units in Germany. These aircraft plus the six 416 Squadron aircraft from Doha returned to Canada on 17 and 18 March.

Canadian CF-18s had no contacts with Iraqi aircraft in the air. The only engagement with the enemy took place in late February when in the middle of the night two CF-18s were called to assist two USN aircraft which were engaging an Iraqi-Exocet-equipped TNC-45 patrol boat. The CF-18s fired a Sparrow missile which missed, but were able to hit the boat with gunfire. After a new attack by Navy aircraft the boat was sunk. In all, 34 CF-18s were deployed to the Gulf, with a maximum of 24 in theatre at any one time. The CF-18s flew 5,730hr (and the Boeing 707, 306hr). No Hornets were damaged. 439 Squadron (augmented) returned to Baden-Söllingen on 5 March 1991, until January 1993 when they returned to Canada via Prestwick. Baden-Söllingen closed on 20 January.

Additional Information:

★ On 7 December 1992 the US Navy signed a $3.715 billion development contract for the F/A-18E/F Hornet upgrade. The cost-plus-incentive contract covers 7½ years of engineering and support activities, including the manufacture of five single-seat 'E' and two dual-seat 'F' models plus three ground test articles.

★ On 5 June 1992 the Finnish Minister of Defence signed a Letter of Offer and Acceptance in the sale of 64 F/A-18 Hornet fighters, including 57 F/A-18Cs and seven F/A-18Ds. Deliveries will begin in late 1995 and continue through 2000.

★ VMA(AW)-533 was redesignated VMFA(AW)-533 on 1 October 1992 as the 4th Marine Corps F/A-18D squadron. Before receiving their first Hornet, the unit was moved to MCAS Beaufort, SC. The other MCAS Cherry Point based A-6E units will move to Beaufort as well before converting to the F/A-18D. They are VMA(AW)-224 and 332.

★ VMFA-333 and 531 were deactivated at MCAS Beaufort and MCAS El Toro respectively on 31 March 1992.

★ VMFA-112 at NAS Dallas started conversion from the F-4S to the F/A-18A and B in the Fall of 1992.

★ VAQ-34 at NAS Lemoore will have been disestablished by 1 October 1993 with the EW agressor role going to the US Navy/Reserve.

★ VFA-127 at NAS Fallon added six F/A-18A Hornets to its fleet of 16 F-5E/Fs in 1992. The 'Desert Bogeys' mission is combat training of Hornet pilots and support of the Strike Warfare Center

F/A-18A (163166, 'DR-05)   VMFA-312, MCAS Beaufort, SC
F/A-18A (163149, DR-08)   VMFA-312, MCAS Beaufort, SC
The sixth and final MAG-31 F-4S squadron at MCAS Beaufort, SC,
that converted to the F/A-18 Hornet was Marine Fighter Attack
Squadron (VMFA)-312. They became operational as a Hornet
squadron in July 1988.

VMF-312 was commissioned on 1 June 1943 at Page Field, SC,
with 10 SNJ-4 Texans and a single F4Y-1D Corsair. After
assignment to MAG-11, receiving 24 Goodyear FG-1 Corsairs, the
'Checkerboards' operated from the captured Kadena airstrip until
the war's end. Altogether 59.5 combat kills had been accounted for.
From March-June 1951, VMF-312 flew assigned escort and
blockade missions against North Korea from the light carrier
Bataan. Some 4,945 accident-free hours of carrier operations were
amassed while logging 1,920 carrier landings. Via the F-9F, FJ-2,
FJ-3 and F-8U-1, the squadron received the F-4B in February 1966
and was consequently redesignated VMFA-312. The squadron
relocated from Beaufort to MCAS Cherry Point, NC, on 15 February
1971, but moved back south on 1 September 1974. VMFA-312 is
the oldest operational fighter squadron in the Marine Corps. In July
1990 VMFA-312 deployed for six months to MCAS Iwakuni in Japan
under the Unit Deployment Program and relieved VMFA-122 on
17 July. In its turn in April 1991 VMFA-122 relieved the
'Checkerboards', who had had to extend their stay at Iwakuri to
nine months because of the situation in the Persian Gulf. Four
months later — on 8 August — VMFA-321 received their first three
F/A-18C attack Hornets.

Left:
Aircraft 05 is carrying an AGM-88A HARM on the pylon under the
left wing and an AIM-9L on the left wingtip launch rail. The AGM-
88A HARM (High-Speed Anti-Radiation Missile) has a higher speed,
longer range, faster reaction and a more destructive warhead than
its predecessors Shrike and Standard Anti-Radiation missiles.
Under the right wing the aircraft carries an AGM-84A Harpoon air-
to-surface anti-shipping missile. HARMs were frequently used
against Iraqi air defence radar installations and SAM sites.   *US Navy*

Right:
It is a common practice in the Marine Corps that after returning
from a mission, aircraft make a 'hot' refuel stop before progressing
to their spot on the flightline.   *Theo van Geffen, IAAP*

Left and Above:

F/A-18A (161964, DW-03) VMFA-251, MCAS Beaufort, SC
F/A-18A (163165, DW-12) VMFA-251, MCAS Beaufort, SC

'*Custos Caelorum*' — or 'Guardians of the sky' — is the motto of
VMFA-251 'Thunderbolts', the third squadron at MCAS Beaufort,
SC, that converted from the venerable F-4S Phantom to the F/A-18
Hornet.

   The first local F/A-18 flight was made by the CO on 17 June 1986
in aircraft 161965, which had been received from VFA-106, NAS
Cecil Field. The 'Thunderbolts' were declared operational on
25 August 1986. For the period 1 June 1988-31 May 1989, VMFA-
251 received the (USMC) Commandant's Aviation Efficiency Trophy

in recognition of 'the squadron's outstanding performance in flight
safety, accident prevention, combat readiness and overall
participation in Naval Aviation competition'. The unit completed
seven years and 30,000 accident-free flying hours on 5 April 1990.

   VMFA-251 was formed in North Island, Ca, in 1944 as VMO-251.
The role was reconnaissance and observation, flying the F-4F
Wildcat. On 31 October 1964 the 'Thunderbolts' received the F-4B
followed in June 1971 by the F-4J. Later the unit became the first
Marine squadron to convert to the slatted wing F-4S.

   The 'DW' unit code is carried in the inner surface of the fin,
making enough room on the other surface for the distinguishing
lightning flash. *Both: Theo van Geffen, IAAP*

F/A-18A (162454, VE-01) VMFA-115, MCAS Beaufort, SC
F/A-18A (162465, VE-12) VMFA-115, MCAS Beaufort, SC
The second Marine Corps Air Station (MCAS) to convert to the
F/A-18 was Beaufort in South Carolina. The station houses six
Hornet units, which are controlled by Marine Aircraft Group
(MAG)-31, which reports directly to 2 MAW at MCAS Cherry Point,
NC. MAG-31 has been stationed at Beaufort since 1 November
1961. Its role is to conduct anti-air warfare and offensive air
support operations in support of Fleet Marine Forces from
advanced bases, expeditionary airfields or aircraft carriers.

The 'Silver Eagles' were organised in Santa Barbara, Ca in July
1943 as VMF-115, flying the F-4U Corsair. In the Korean War,
VMF-115 flew 9,250 combat sorties. In following years transition
was made to the F-6A Skyray and VMF-115 became VMF(AW)-115.
On receipt of the F-4B in January 1964 the squadron was
redesignated VMFA-115. From October 1965 to March 1971 the
'Silver Eagles' were stationed in South Vietnam, completing 35,000

combat sorties. In July 1977 the unit was relocated from MCAS
Iwakuni to Beaufort, flying the F-4J at that time. The last flight in
the F-4S was made on 14 December 1984. Training in the F/A-18
was received at NAS Cecil Field, Fl from the Navy East Coast Fleet
Replacement Squadron, VFA-106. The first two Hornets were
received on 3 July 1985, and the C-1 status (combat ready) was
achieved on 28 January 1986. In mid-1991 VMFA-115 had achieved
30,000 accident-free flying hours.

Marine Corps units stationed in CONUS (Continental United
States) participate in the Unit Deployment Program (UDP) at MCAS
Iwakuni, Japan. Normally, two Hornet squadrons are involved and
deployed at the same time. During their six-month stay at Iwakuni,
units are assigned to Marine Aircraft Group (MAG)-15. In mid-July
1989, VMFA-115 ferried its 12 Hornets to Iwakuni and replaced
VMFA-333. VMFA-115 in its turn was replaced by VMFA-122 in
January 1990, taking over the squadron's Hornets.
Both: Theo van Geffen, IAAP

Above and Right:

F/A-18A (162398, VW-00; 163144, VW-10)   VMFA-314, MCAS El Toro, Ca

Marine Fighter Attack Squadron (VMFA)-314 'Black Knights' at MCAS El Toro, Ca, was the first operational squadron in the US Marine Corps — beating the US Navy — to convert to the F/A-18 Hornet. They became operational as an F/A-18 squadron on 7 January 1983, during ceremonies at MCAS El Toro, which also marked the official start of Hornet flight operations at the station. Squadron personnel had received training since August 1982 from VFA-125 at NAS Lemoore, Ca. The first Hornet arrived on 15 December 1982.

Commissioned on 1 October 1943 and flying the F-4U Corsair, VMFA-314 was the first MAW-3 unit to convert to jet aircraft, the F-9F Panther in 1952. This was followed in October 1961 by another 'first': it became the first Marine squadron to convert to the F-4B Phantom. In early 1966 the 'Black Knights' made the move to Da Nang, South Vietnam, where more than 28,000 combat sorties were flown.

VMFA-314 was part of Carrier Air Wing (CVW)-13 aboard USS *Coral Sea* (CV-43) between October 1985 and May 1986. In March and April 1986 the 'Black Knights' participated in actions against Libya: Combat Air Patrols (CAP) and SAM suppression missions were flown, meaning the combat début for both the Hornet and the AGM-88A HARM. VMFA-314 won the CNO aviation safety 'S' for CY-90.

The photographs show F/A-18As of VMFA-314 after flying a DACT mission against F-16A/B Fighting Falcons of Oregon ANG's 114 TFTS in late April 1990. F/A-18s from El Toro are frequent visitors to Kingsley Field, Or. *Both Theo van Geffen, IAAP*

Right:

F/A-18B (161249, 01)
USNTPS, NAS Patuxent
River, Md
The US Naval Test Pilot
School is stationed at
NAS Patuxent River, Md. The
School was established in
1958 and its task is to train
experienced Naval pilots,
Naval Flight Officers, US Army
helicopter pilots, foreign
students and engineers, to
become fully qualified test
pilots, test flight officers and
test project engineers. Some
68 graduates are produced
annually from two concurrent
classes. A class takes 11
months of instruction
consisting of specific fixed-
wing, rotary-wing and
airborne systems curricula.
Aircraft types include the A-
4M, TA-7C, T-2C and U-6A.

The photograph shows F/A-
18B of the TPS in a splendid
white and red colour scheme,
quite a contrast to the present
operational 'colours'. The F/A-
18B has proven to be
extremely useful in
demonstration of the high
angle of attack handling.
Dave Ostrowski via AIR

Above right:

F/A-18A (161925, 7T-156)   NATC, NAS Patuxent River, Md
F/A-18A (160782, 7T-151)   NATC, NAS Patuxent River, Md
Patuxent River Naval Air Station was born of an effort to centralise
widely dispersed air testing facilities established during the pre-
World War 2 years. Flight test operations started in 1942, within a
year of the first turf being dug. By the end of 1944, the Station had
formed the Service Test, Electronics Test, Flight Test and Tactical
Test Divisions. The Naval Air Test Center (NATC) was established as
a separate entity on 16 June 1945, organisationally dividing the test
and support functions. The first US test of the adaptability of jet
aircraft to shipboard operations was conducted by NATC in 1946,
when an FH-1 Phantom was flown aboard USS *Franklin D.
Roosevelt*.

A sweeping reorganisation took place in 1975. Under the plan,
Flight Test, Service Test and Weapons Systems Test Divisions were
disestablished and were replaced by Strike Aircraft, Antisubmarine
Aircraft, Rotary Wing Aircraft and Systems Engineering Test

Directorates. NATC is the Naval Air Systems Command's principal
site for development testing. The Strike Aircraft Test Directorate
(SATD) tests experimental and production fixed wing, attack, fighter
and other specifically designated aircraft, by technical analysis of
characteristics exhibited on the ground, aboard ships and in flight.
Test programmes include monitoring contractor development of
fighter and attack aircraft, support and participation in contractor
full scale development (FSD) tests. Major programme involvement
includes F/A-18, F-14B, F-14D and AV-8B. A Marine Aviation
Detachment (MAD) at Patuxent River supports the Navy and Marine
Corps' projects in the various NATC Directorates. The NATC was
disestablished by 1 January 1992 and consolidated within the
NAWC (the Naval Air Warfare Center) in a massive plan to
streamline and restructure the Navy's Research, Development, Test
and Evaluation establishments. One of NAWC's major divisions, the
Aircraft Division, is located at NAS Patuxent River. The division is
responsible for aircraft, engines, avionics and aircraft support.
Dave Ostrowski, via AIR/US Navy

Left:

F/A-18A (161366, XF-25) VX-4, NAS Point Mugu, Ca

Air Test and Evaluation Squadron Four (VX-4) at NAS Point Mugu, Ca, tests aircraft weapons systems and support equipment in the environments in which they will be used. The 'Evaluators' also develop tactics and doctrine for Fleet uses of these weapons and associated support systems. VX-4 has evaluated most of the Navy's air-launched guided missiles. The unit continues to evaluate the expanded performance capabilities of the Phoenix missile and its related weapon systems under various threat conditions. The squadron was the first Navy squadron to operate and maintain the Hornet, and has conducted the F/A-18 Operational Test and Evaluation (OPEVAL) at various test sites throughout the USA. The first Hornet was received in February 1981.

In this photograph a F/A-18A Hornet of VX-4 is readied for a launch off the first catapult aboard USS *Carl Vinson*.
Don Linn, via AIR

Left:

F/A-18A (161744, AD-323) VFA-106, NAS Cecil Field, Fl

Before VFA-106 'Gladiators' was re-established at NAS Cecil Field, Fl, on 27 April 1984 as the F/A-18 Hornet Atlantic Fleet Replacement Squadron — making the beginning of East Coast transition training of F-4 and A-7 squadrons to the Hornet — all Hornet–related training of pilots and aircraft maintenance personnel for both the US Marine Corps and Navy had been carried out at NAS Lemoore, Ca, by VFA-125.

The 'Gladiators' were originally established as Fighter-Bomber Squadron 17 in January 1945. After completion of combat operations in Korea, the squadron was designated Attack Squadron 106. VA-106 was involved in the catastrophic fire aboard USS *Forrestal* on 29 July 1967, which destroyed or damaged over half of the squadron's A-4 Skyhawks. The unit was disestablished on 7 November 1969. The 'Gladiators' achieved several milestones, including the achievement of over 80,000 accident-free flying hours in early 1990, and the attainment of an unparalleled 100% pilot qualification.

VFA-106 has 60 F/A-18s assigned, including the C and D model. The squadron was the first Fleet Training Squadron to receive the F/A-18C.

This photographs shows a VFA-106 F/A-18A being pushed back manually during carrier qualifications aboard USS *America*.
Don Spering, AIR

Above:

F/A-18A (162871, AG-305) VFA-136, USS Dwight D. Eisenhower
When the USS *Dwight D. Eisenhower* (CVN-69) departed Norfolk, Va, on 8 March 1990 to relieve the USS *Forrestal* in the Mediterranean for a routine deployment, its Carrier Air Wing Seven included two types of aircraft in their first major deployment: the S-3B Viking with VS-31 and the F-14A (Plus) since redesignated F-14B with VF-142 and VF-143.

The deployment was to become a very dramatic one. The carrier participated in the evacuation of foreign nationals from war-plagued Monrovia, Liberia. Just after the invasion of Kuwait by Iraq the 'Ike' received orders to sail through the Suez Canal to the Persian Gulf. The ship returned to Norfolk, Va, on 12 September 1990 after having been relieved late in August by USS *Saratoga*. The Hornet components of CVW-7 are VFA-131 'Wildcats' and VFA-136 'Knighthawks'. VFA-136 was established at NAS Lemoore,

Ca on 1 July 1985. The 'Knighthawks' made the move to Cecil Field in March 1986 and joined CVW-13 three months later. It made its first cruise from 29 September 1987 to 29 March 1988. Since then, VFA-131 and 136 joined CVW-7 aboard the 'Ike'. The 'Knighthawks' were the 1989 winners of the Cecil Field Silver Bombs award for air-to-ground excellence. On 10 April 1990, Lt-Cdr Randy Causey of VFA-136 recorded the one millionth flying hour of the F/A-18. The achievement comes just seven years after the Hornet reached operational capability with the Navy in March 1983, and combines flying hours for all F/A-18 operators, including NASA. Lt-Cdr Causey, who recorded his 1,000th Hornet flying hour, had been launched from USS *Dwight D. Eisenhower* in the Mediterranean.

CVW-7's two F/A-18 units traded their As in for the C model, after returning from their 1990 trip. The 'Knighthawks' received their first C on 13 November 1990. *US Navy (Lt-Cdr John Leenhouts)*

F/A-18As (161523, One; 161520, Two; 161521, Three; 161524, Four) 'Blue Angels', NAS Pensacola, Fl

The US Navy Flight Demonstration Team 'Blue Angels' gives some 75 shows every year, completing some 125,000 miles. Since the formation of the team in 1946, more than 210 million people have watched the 'Blue Angels'. Although its home station is NAS Pensacola, Fl, quite a bit of time is being spent at NAS El Centro, Ca, to undertake pre-season work-up training. To accomplish its mission, the 'Blue Angels' have nine F/A-18s assigned, eight F/A-18s and a single F/A-18B. The As are numbered 1-6, 8 and 9, and the B number 7. The single-seaters are frequently re-numbered throughout the demo season. The aircraft — early production F/A-18s with the gun removed — are no longer suitable for carrier operations. They are equipped with civilian ILS and navigation equipment, a smoke generating system and new flight control system software, optimised for aerobatics. The announcement of converting from the A-4F to the F/A-18 was made on 24 February 1986. The changeover to the Hornet marked the 17th consecutive year in which the US Navy has flown McDonnell Douglas-built aeroplanes in the 'Blue Angels' squadron. The first 'Blue Angels' F/A-18 was modified by McDonnell Douglas, the remainder by NARF (Naval Air Rework Facility) at North Island. Training in the aircraft started in January 1987 at NAS El Centro. The first airshow using the F/A-18 was given on 25 April 1987. The squadron was renamed Navy Flight Demonstration Squadron on 1 December 1973. *Frank Mormillo*

F/A-18A (161366) 'Blue Angels', NAS Pensacola, Fl

F/A-18A Six, one of the two solos, performs during the open house at NAS Miramar in August 1988. The wing surfaces are partly covered by condensation vapour.
US Navy (PH1 Bruce R. Trombecky)

Above:

F/A-18D (163434)   McDonnell Douglas Corp, St Louis, Mo
This photograph shows the prototype of the F/A-18D Night Attack
Hornet making a test flight along the banks of the Mississippi river.
The first flight of the type (there is no difference in designation as
to Ds, with or without night attack capabilities) was made from the
company's airfield in St Louis on 6 May 1988. The delivery to the
Navy of the first production Night Attack F/A-18 took place on
1 November 1989, the receiver being NATC (Naval Air Test Center)
at NAS Patuxent River, Md, for further evaluation. The US Navy will
use the twin-seat F/A-18s as trainers, although the Ds are delivered
to the Navy with two stationary hand controls to operate the
weapons systems. These are used by Marine Corps backseaters
instead of the stick and throttle; a modification kit is provided to
the Navy allowing the installation of conventional flight controls in
the rear cockpit.

The F/A-18D will also be used by the US Marine Corps, which will
re-equip its VMA(AW) squadrons with the type, transferring the
A-6E Intruders to the US Navy. The D version of the Hornet will also
replace the RF-4B Phantom and the OA-4/TA-4 Skyhawk. The type
provides the MAGFT (Marine Air-Ground Task Force) with a platform
capable of tactical reconnaissance and tactical air control, while
retaining the offensive and defensive anti-air capabilities of the
F/A-18A and C. Initially, the MC wanted 48 F/A-18Ds, but this
number was later raised to 72. The first unit to receive the new
aircraft was VMFA(AW)-121 'Green Knights' at MCAS El Toro on
11 May 1990. *McDonnell Douglas*

Above:

The cockpit in Night Attack F/A-18C and two-seat D model Hornets
has three multipurpose colour display screens, including a colour
digital moving map, and an improved head-up display. Images from
the aircraft's forward-looking infra-red navigation sensor are
projected on to the head-up display and allow pilots to see through
the dark. Through a minor (software) upgrade and the addition of
beacon mode bombing, the F/A-18D is receiving an all-weather
close-support capability. *McDonnell Douglas*

Above:

***F/A-18A (162890, NF-202) VFA-151, USS** Midway*

VFA-151 is one of the only two US Navy F-4 units which converted to the F/A-18 Hornet. In that process, VF-151 was redesignated VFA-151 on 17 June 1986. Strike Fighter Squadron 151 was originally commissioned Fighter Squadron 23 in 1948 at NAS Oceana, Va. In February 1959, VF-23 became VF-151. Five years later the 'Vigilantes' converted to the F-4 Phantom and made a total of seven cruises to Yankee Station in the Gulf of Tonkin. During the seventh cruise (aboard USS *Midway*), VF-151 spent 205 days in combat operations, flew over 2,500 sorties and delivered nearly three million pounds of ordnance.

On 30 June 1973, CVW-5 and its units moved to NAF Atsugi, Japan, which would be used as its forward deployment base. In September, VF-151 and its sister squadron VF-161, exchanged their F-4Ns for the F-4Js which were received from VF-191 and 194 when the USS *Coral Sea* returned to Alameda, Ca. From the F-4J the squadron converted to the upgraded F-4S. In 1988 the

'Vigilantes' completed 32,000 accident-free flying hours over a period of eight years.

Before CVW-5's Strike Fighter force returned to NAF Atsugi in October 1986, the squadrons deployed to NAS Fallon, NV, for an intensive training programme. VFA-151 departed NAS Lemoore on 17 November 1986. Refuelled by US Air Force KC-10 and KC-135 tankers, the trip took the 'Vigilantes' to the Far East via NAS Barbers Point, Hi, and NAS Agana. When *Independence* replaced *Midway* as forward-based carrier in Yokusuka on 25 August 1991, VF-151 stayed on *Midway.* The 'Vigilantes' arrived back at NAS Lemoore on 11 September 1991 and were assinged to Commander, Strike Fighter Wing, US Pacific Fleet until assignment to CVW-2 and USS *Constellation.* The first deployment is not scheduled unitl spring 1993. *Mike Grove via AIR*

Carrier Air Wing 14 (CVW-14) aboard the USS *Constellation* was the first Air Wing to deploy with the F/A-18 Hornet. It was also the first ever deployment of a carrier with F-14 Tomcats and Hornets, making the wing the most modern and powerful one in the world. The CVW's Strike Fighter components comprise VFA-25 and VFA-113, the US Navy's first deployed F/A-18 squadrons. The 'Stingers', originally designated as VF-113, formed in July 1948, flying the F-4U Corsair. After conversions to the Cougar and Panther, VF-113 was redesignated VA-113 in March 1956 and re-equipped with the A-4 Skyhawk. The year 1965 brought the 'Stingers' to combat in South East Asia, flying the A-4C from the deck of USS *Enterprise*.

In December 1968 the unit converted to the A-7 and completed six combat cruises in South East Asia as part of CVW-2 aboard the USS *Ranger*. The US Navy's Strike Fighter era began on 25 March 1983 when VA-113 was redesignated VFA-113. The last mission with the A-7E was flown on 23 March 1983. The first F/A-18A was received by the 'Stingers' on 16 August 1983 and the transition was completed on 14 December 1983.

The 'Stingers' last mishap occurred in 1974 when the squadron was flying the A-7E Corsair II. It meant the start of the longest accident-free streak in the history of Navy and Marine Corps tactical aviation, running in September 1991 to an unbelievable 17.5 years and 76,000 flying hours, of which 36,000 have been with the Hornet. In 1989, VFA-113 won the Chief of Naval Operations Safety Award, Safety 'S'. During that year's cruise aboard USS *Constellation*, the squadron flew over 4,300hr and logged more than 1,300 carrier landings, all without a single mishap.

CVW-14's last combat deployment was made on board USS *Independence* (CV-62). The *'Indy'* sailed on 23 June 1990 on what should have become a routine deployment to the Western Pacific and Indian Ocean, but in August the Iraqi invasion of Kuwait changed these plans considerably. The ship received orders to sail to the Gulf of Oman and stayed on station for three months. On 1 October *Independence* entered the Persian Gulf for a training exercise. This was the first time a US carrier did so since USS *Constellation* in 1974. Relieved by the USS *Midway*, *'Indy'* began the long trek home on 2 November 1990.

VFA-113's sister squadron in the Wing is VFA-25 'Fist of the Fleet'. The squadron is a veteran command in naval aviation. It was commissioned in 1943 as Torpedo Squadron 17 and operated the SB2C attack bomber; through VA-6B and VA-65 it became VA-25 in July 1959. The unit flew the A-1 Skyraider until April 1968, when it started conversion to the A-7B. Four of VA-25's A-1s made history on 20 June 1965, when they shot down a North Vietnamese MiG-17 while on a ResCap mission without fighter protection. The A-7E was received two years later and the type was flown through the spring of 1983. At that time the first VA-25 pilots began training on the F/A-18. Redesignation to VFA-25 followed on 1 July 1983. The full complement of 12 aircraft was reached by March 1984. In mid-1987, VFA-25 had accumulated 55,000 accident free flying hours in a 12-year period. During the December 1988-June 1989 deployment on board the USS *Constellation,* the 'Fists' were awarded their second consecutive Battle Efficiency 'E' award and the CNO Safety 'S' award. In addition VFA-25 also received the Capt Michael J. Estocin award for 1988. This also gave VFA-25 unprecedented acknowledgement as the 'Triple Crown' winner for the US Navy Strike Fighter community.

After arriving home on 20 December 1990 the squadron did not stand down, but emphasised combat readiness through flying an increased number of sorties in preparation for a possible departure to the Gulf region. On 11 September 1991 the 'Fists' and the 'Stingers' arrived at NAS Lemoore and prepared themselves to convert to F/A-18Cs, with a night strike capability. VFA-113 received its first F/A-18CN on 18 October, VFA-25 followed two weeks later. Eventually CVW-14 will be assigned to USS *Carl Vinson* (CVN-70).

Above right:
F/A-18s (161936, -307; -305; -306)   VFA-113, USS Constellation. *McDonnell Douglas*

Right:
F/A-18A (NK-300)   VFA-113, USS Constellation NK-300, sporting the colours of its Air Wing Commander, refuels from a KA-6D of VA-196. *Naval Aviation News*

Left and Above:

F/A-18A (163126, AC-303) VFA-15, USS Theodore Roosevelt
F/A-18A VFA-15, USS Theodore Roosevelt

The 'Valions' will celebrate their 50th anniversary on 10 January 1992, making them one of the oldest squadrons in the US Navy. They were established as Torpedo Squadron Four (VT-4) aboard USS *Ranger* on 10 January 1942 flying the SBD Dauntless. Other aircraft flown since its inception were the TBM Avenger, AD-4 Spad and A-4. Transition to the Skyhawk was made between August and November 1965, although original plans had called for a transition to the A-6 Intruder. Via the A-7B in June 1969, the E model of the Corsair II was received of October 1975. While embarked aboard USS *Independence* in November 1980, VA-15 saw extensive sea-going action, while on station off Lebanon during the Israeli-Syrian missile crisis. Three years later the 'Valions' were back in the region, this time as a part of the multi-national Peace Keeping

Force. On 4 December 1983, the unit made a successful air strike against Syrian targets in Lebanon. The last A-7E mission was flown on 25 August 1986. Redesignation from Attack Squadron to Strike Fighter Squadron took place on 1 October 1986. The first Hornet was received in January 1987. One month later the 'Valions' received Cecil Field's 100th F/A-18 (c/n 163124, AC-302).

The year 1990 marked the sixth consecutive year with zero mishaps, equating to 21,000 accident free flying hours. Also 1990 marked the fourth consecutive year the 'Valions' won the Light Attack Wing One dive bombing derby. The USS *Theodore Roosevelt* received orders in December 1990 to deploy with its Carrier Air Wing to the Red Sea to supplement the carriers already in the area. After the outbreak of hostilities against Iraq in January 1991, aircraft of CVW-8 became heavily involved in striking at Iraqi positions in both Kuwait and Iraq. *Both McDonnell Douglas*

Left and Right:

F/A-18C (163465, AB-314) VFA-82, USS America
F/A-18C (163461, AB-410) VFA-86, USS America
The Strike Fighter component of CVW-1 aboard USS America consists of Strike Fighter Squadrons (VFA)-82 and 86. When not at sea, the squadrons are stationed at NAS Cecil Field, Fl, and managed by CLAW-1 (Commander Light Attack Wing One) who, in turn, reports directly to the Commander Strike Fighter Wings Atlantic.

VFA-82's history goes back to 1 April 1944, when it was established as Fighter Squadron 82 based at NAS Atlantic City, NJ. At that time the unit flew F6F Hellcats. VF-82 was disbanded on 15 April 1959. On 1 May 1967 it was reformed as Attack Squadron 82, flying 12 A-7As as part of CVW-6 aboard USS America. After one year of training, the 'Marauders' deployed to the waters of South East Asia and participated in air strikes against North Vietnam. In August 1970, conversion to the A-7E began. After returning from its final deployment aboard USS Nimitz with CVW-8 in June 1987, VA-82 converted to the F/A-18 on 6 November 1987, becoming the first Fleet Squadron to receive the C model. VA-82 was redesignated VFA-82 on 13 July 1987 and in February 1990 it flew west as part of CVW-9 (Composite) to escort USS Constellation around the Horn of South America to SLEP in Philadelphia, Pa. During the deployment, the 'Marauders' were informed that they had won the Battle 'E' award.

VFA-86 traces its origins to the Korean War. In the early 1950s, Fighter Squadron 921 was stationed at NAS St Louis, Mo. While deployed to Guantanamo Bay, Cuba, in 1953, the squadron was redesignated as VF-84. Two years later a further redesignation to VA-86 followed after transition to the F7U-3M Cutlass. On 1 June 1967, VA-86 became the Fleet's first operational A-7A squadron. Over the years, VA-86 has received six COMNAVAIRLANT Battle 'Es'. On 1 July 1987 the unit was officially redesignated VFA-86.

Arriving in the Red Sea on 16 January 1991, USS America brought the number of carriers in the area to four. Aircraft of the wing participated in the massive air strikes against Iraqi targets in Kuwait and Iraq flying 3,000+ sorties. The carrier returned to Norfolk, Va on 18 April. *Both McDonnell Douglas*

the largest aviation unit in the Navy. VA-125 trained over 700 A-7A/B/C FRPs and 5,500 FMPs. With the introduction of the Hornet into the US Navy, Fighter Attack Squadron 125 was commissioned as the first dual mission squadron at Lemoore on 13 November 1980. For this occasion, F/A-18A c/n 161216 had been specially painted as NJ-501. Before commission, the initial cadre of VFA-125 had been an integral part of the F/A-18 fleet introduction team. Factory training of 20 pilots had commenced in January 1981. Each pilot received extensive academic instruction by McDonnell Douglas instructors in system operation and 10hr of hands-on training in the F/A-18 design simulator, which was available prior to the delivery of the aircraft. VFA-125 was the first of three planned F/A-18 Strike Fighter Replacement Squadrons. Before the Marine Corps started its own Hornet training, personnel were trained at Lemoore. Hence the fact that the CO of VFA-125 was from the Navy and the Executive Officer from the Corps. The right fuselage of VFA-125s Hornets shows Marine Corps markings, and the left side Navy markings.

The first F/A-18A was received on 19 February 1981 (from VX-4), while the first F/A-18B arrived on 10 March 1981. In March 1983 VFA-125's name changed to Strike Fighter Squadron, reflecting the increased capability that the Hornet provides to the Carrier Air Wing. By March 1985, VFA-125 had amassed over 30,000 flying hours in the F/A-18, all accident free. VFA-125 averages some 1,500 flying hours monthly in the A, B, C and D models of the Hornet, and trains approximately 120 pilots and 3,500 maintenance crews each year. Pilots from the US Navy, US Marine Corps, Canadian Armed Forces, Royal Australian Air Force and Spanish Air Force have been trained by VFA-125. Kuwaiti AF pilots also receive training at NAS Lemoore. Operations at Lemoore are supplemented with air-to-air and air-to-ground training detachments to MCAS Yuma, Az, and NAS Fallon. *McDonnell Douglas*

Above:
F/A-18A (161748, NJ-511) VFA-125, NAS Lemoore, Ca
The entire Strike Fighter Community of the Pacific Fleet falls under COMLATWINGPAC (Commander, Light Attack Wing, US Pacific Fleet), which is located at NAS Lemoore and also encompasses NAS Alameda, Ca, and NAS Fallon, Nv. It exercises functional command of the West Coast F/A-18 Fleet Readiness Squadron, VFA-125 'Rough Raiders'.

VA-125 was disbanded on 1 October 1977 after almost 20 years of service as the backbone of the Light Attack Community on the US Pacific coast. Its mission had been the combat readiness training of Fleet Replacement Pilots (FRP) and Fleet Replacement Aircraft Maintenance Personnel (FMP). Until the introduction of the A-7A Corsair II on 25 September 1969, VA-125 flew all the models of the A-4 Skyhawk. During this period the squadron had over 100 A-4s and 1,000 officers and enlisted personnel assigned, making it

Right:
F/A-18B (161704, NJ-533) VFA-125, NAS Lemoore, Ca
On this photograph, taken from the Landing Signal Officer (LSO) platform, a VFA-125 F/A-18B is about to catch one of the wires aboard the deck of USS *Carl Vinson* (CVN-70) during carrier qualification. Note the empty back-seat. Navy two-seat B and D training Hornets are used solely by the two Fleet Replacement Squadrons, VFA-106 at NAS Cecil Field, Fl, and VFA-125 at NAS Lemoore, Ca. *Don Linn, via AIR*

Below:

F/A-18A (ND-505) 161756 VFA-305, NAS Point Mugu, Ca
The second F/A-18-equipped unit within CVWR-30 is VFA-305
'Lobos', stationed at NAS Point Mugu, Ca. Its relationship with the
Hornet started on 18 January 1987, when Attack Squadron 305 was
redesignated Strike Fighter Squadron 305, receiving its first F/A-18
eight days later. VFA-305's mission is to maintain full combat
readiness at all times so that in case of a national emergency it
could be called up to join the Naval Air Forces of the Pacific and
Atlantic Fleets.

Commissioned as Attack Squadron 305 on 1 July 1970 at NAS
Los Alamitos, Ca, the squadron began its operations flying the A-4C
Skyhawk. In January 1971, after transferring to NAS Point Mugu,
the 'Lobos' traded in their A-4s for the LTV A-7A on 26 June 1972.
VA-305 operated the Corsair II for 15 years, which included a
transition to the A-7B in 1978. The highlight of 1988 was the

'Lobos'' first F/A-18 carrier qualification trials aboard
USS *Constellation*, which culminated in the squadron's outstanding
success in deploying with CVWR-30 aboard USS *Enterprise*. In early
1991, VFA-305 surpassed 54,000 consecutive accident-free flying
hours, amassed in more than 14 years of flying

The 'Lobos' were part of CVW-11 (Composite) on board the USS
Abraham Lincoln (CVN-72), when the carrier departed Norfolk, Va
on 25 September 1990 on its 22,000-mile transit around South
America to its new homeport Alameda, Ca arriving on 20 November
1990. The squadron's detachment consisted of six F/A-18s, 13
pilots and 154 maintenance/administrative personnel. The Hornets
participated in two major air wing strikes against Chilean airfields.
The 'Lobos' won the Golden Tailhook award for the cruise. VFA-305
replaced VA-22 and 94 while these units converted from the A-7E
to the F/A-18C. *Frank B. Mormillo*

Above:

F/A-18A (161735, ND-301) VFA-303, NAS Lemoore, Ca
Like its sister Carrier Air Wing Reserve on the East Coast, CVWR-30 at NAS Alameda, Ca, has two F/A-18-equipped Strike Fighter Squadrons assigned: VFA-303 at NAS Lemoore, Ca, and VFA-305 at NAS Point Mugu, Ca.

As had happened in April 1971 with the introduction of the A-7 Corsair II into the US Naval Reserve, the 'Golden Hawks' became the first US Navy Reserve unit to convert to the F/A-18 Hornet, receiving the majority of its aircraft from VMFA-531. In this respect it had been redesignated as VFA-303 on 1 January 1984, making the move to Lemoore at the same time, and had received its first Hornet on 19 October 1985. The transfer of F/A-18s to the USNR was part of a plan to introduce more modern aircraft in the Reserve forces.

The squadron was originally commissioned at NAS Alameda, Ca, on 1 April 1970 and equipped with the A-4C, although its history

dates back to 1945 when a Naval Reserve Group was organised at Livermore, Ca. In 1948, when the Group was divided into squadrons, the unit was designated Attack Squadron 876, flying the F-4U Corsair and afterwards the F-2F Banshee. VA-303 traded in its A-7As for the B model in 1978 and lost its last A-7B in October 1983, awaiting the arrival of the F/A-18 Hornet. Organisationally and operationally, VFA-303 — like other USNR units — closely parallels active duty fleet squadrons with training requirements that include all phases of combat strike fighter tactics and carrier operations.

In this respect VFA-303 together with the other units of CVWR-30 spent two weeks in August 1990 on board the USS *Nimitz* during Active Duty Training (ADT). The mission for the Air Wing units was to learn to operate and function as a single unit. The 'Golden Hawks' made some 190 traps and accumulated a similar number of flying hours. VFA-303 has recently accumulated 47,020 accident-free flying hours over a 16-year period. *Theo van Geffen, IAAP*

The National Aeronautics and Space Administration's (NASA) Ames Research Center at Dryden Flight Research Facility, Edwards AFB, flies six F/A-18As and one F/A-18B, which are on a long-term loan from the US Navy. The first Hornet was received in October 1984 and the final one in December 1989. Most aircraft were drawn from the pre-production and early production F/A-18s. Five As and the B model are used as chase and support aircraft and pilot proficiency training, replacing the F-104s. The Hornets are better qualified for the agile close-support work than the Starfighter.

The first F/A-18 received by NASA (840/160780) is used in the High Angle of Attack (HAOA) Program. 'Angle of Attack' (or 'Alpha') is an engineering term for the angle of an aircraft's body and wings relative to its actual flight path. The ultimate aim of the programme is to allow a HAOA of at least 70° through a thrust vectoring system, resulting in increased manoeuvrability, and in making high-performance aircraft safer to fly. The first phase of the study commenced in 1986 and involved more than 100 research flights at up to 55° angle-of-attack. The second phase started in the late summer of 1990, and continued through until the end of the summer of 1991.

Bottom left:
F/A-18A (840/160780) NASA, Edwards AFB, Ca
This photograph taken in March 1990 shows NASA's first F/A-18A Hornet 840/160780 being prepared for a landing at Edwards AFB, Ca. It has just completed a research mission in a programme to study the air flow over the aircraft during high angles of attack in order to validate computer codes and wind tunnel results.
NASA

Above left:
F/A-18A (843/161250) NASA, Edwards AFB, Ca
The flightline at the Dryden Flight Research Facility shows F/A-18A 843/161250 and F/A-18B 845/160781. A glycol-based liquid, released through very small holes around the nose of the Hornet, aids researchers in flow visualisation studies; 843 shows the airflow pattern at about 30° of attack. *NASA*

Facing page:
F/A-18A (840/160780) NASA, Edwards AFB, Ca
In the HAOA research programme, smoke generators and yarn tufts are used on NASA's F/A-18A 840/160780. The aircraft is at about 30° angle of attack. The HAOA programme is conducted jointly with NASA's Langley Research Center.
NASA

Left:

F/A-18C (163706, 64)   PMTC, NAS Point Mugu, Ca
The Pacific Missile Test Center is the Navy's primary facility for air-launched weapons. Other missions include Fleet operations support and training, and electronic warfare projects. PMTC was originally established at NAS Point Mugu, Ca, as the Naval Missile Test Center.

PMTC's Sea Test Range comprises a fully-instrumented 35,000sq mile area about 125 miles by 250 miles long. To carry out its mission, PMTC has a fleet of more than 50 aircraft, many uniquely configured. These include types, such as the F-14 Tomcat, F/A-18 Hornet, RC-12M, EP-3A and RP-3A Orion. PMTC also maintains the largest and most varied inventory of airborne and surface targets in the US Navy, including the QF-4N and QF-86F. It was disestablished on 1 January 1992 when the Navy's RDT&E establishments were streamlined and restructured as a part of a new Command, the NAWC. The NAWC reports to Commander, Naval Air Systems Command and was organised in two major divisions. They are the Aircraft Division, primarily responsible for aircraft, engines, avionics and aircraft support and located at NAS Patuxent River, Md, and the Weapons Division located at NAS Point Mugu primarily responsible for aircraft weapons and weapons systems, simulators and targets. The Weapons Division has operating sites at NAS Point Mugu, China Lake, Albuquerque and White Sands, NM. *Theo van Geffen, IAAP*

Above:
F/A-18C (163738, WT-03)   VMFA-232, Shaikh Isa, Bahrain
At the time of writing, the US Marine Corps possesses four Marine Fighter Attack Squadrons (VMFA), which are equipped with the C version of the F/A-18 Hornet, including VMFA-212, VMFA-232 and VMFA-235. The squadrons are all stationed at MCAS Kaneohe Bay, Hawaii and assigned to Marine Aircraft Group (MAG)-24. In its turn, MAG-24 is assigned to the First Marine Expeditionary Brigade (MEB). Established in the Philippines in 1901, the Brigade relocated to Kaneohe Bay in 1953. The mission is to provide trained, combat-ready air-ground forces capable of executing amphibious assault or other such operations whenever and wherever directed. MAG-24 provides the air support and also comprises five helicopter squadrons, flying CH-46 and CH-53 helicopters.

Before conversion to the F/A-18, the three squadrons flew the F-4S Phantom. The first squadron to lose its Phantoms was VMFA-212 in September 1988. Pilots of the 'Lancers' started training at MCAS El Toro and maintenance personnel headed for NAS Lemoore, Ca. Two months later, VMFA-232 'Red Devils' sent their F-4S aircraft into retirement and began their Hornet orientation. Finally, the 'Death Angels' of VMFA-235 lost their last (and the last active-duty Marine Corps) F-4S on 3 February 1989.

VMFA-212 became operational as an F/A-18C squadron in February 1989, VMFA-232 in May 1989 and VMFA-235 in September 1989, receiving its final two Hornets on 13 November 1989. In connection with the build-up in Operation 'Desert Shield', the three MCAS Kaneohe Bay-based units were deployed to the Gulf area. VMFA-235 deployed on 20 August 1990 and together with VMFA-314, 333 and 451 it was assigned to MAG-70, which was established as initial controlling authority. *US Marine Corps*

Below:

F/A-18C (164030, NG-400) VFA-147, USS Nimitz

During the 2 September 1988-2 March 1989 Westpac/Indian Ocean deployment of USS *Nimitz* (CVN-68), Carrier Air Wing 9's (CVW-9) Attack Squadrons, VA-146 and VA-147 took along their mainstay — the A-7E Corsair II — for the last time. After their return to NAS Lemoore, Ca, the two squadrons started conversion to the F/A-18C Hornet. Their updated A-7s were sent to the remaining A-7 squadrons and Fleet Readiness squadrons.

For about six months, the squadrons were dispersed with personnel going to schools. In a normal training schedule no more than 10% of the squadron's personnel are at school. During conversion it will be upwards of 50% of the maintenance people and pilots in training. VFA-147 was the first Fleet Squadron ever to be commissioned at NAS Lemoore. On 1 February 1967 the

'Argonauts' of VA-147 were also the first A-7A squadron to be formed in the Pacific Fleet and first to deploy in the new aircraft. During the summer of 1969 the unit converted to the A-7E and made the first combat deployment in that aircraft. VA-147 was redesignated VFA-147 on 20 July 1989, with delivery of the first F/A-18C beginning in December. On 3 April 1990, some 30,000 mishap-free flying hours were reached. The USS *Nimitz* and its embarked CVW-9 left the US West Coast on 25 February 1991 to sail to the Persian Gulf area and returned home on 24 August 1991.

McDonnell Douglas

Above:

F/A-18D 164022, VK-06   VMFA(AW)-121, Shaikh Isa, Bahrain
The decision to re-equip the Marine Corps All-Weather Attack Squadrons (VMA[AW]) with the F/A-18D night attack Hornets was based on two reasons: a shortage of A-6E Intruders in the fleet, and to accelerate the reduction of the variety of different types of aircraft in the Marine Corps. In this respect the Hornet would replace the A-6E, OA-4M, RF-4B and TA-4F. The re-equipment plans call for the acquisition of 72 F/A-18Ds of which 48 can be equipped with the Advanced Tactical Reconnaissance System (ATARS), one Marine A-6E squadron converting per FY. Also, that MAG-11 units at MCAS El Toro, Ca, will convert first, while MAG-14 A-6E units at MCAS Cherry Point, NC, participate in the Unit Deployment Plan rotation to MCAS Iwakuni, Japan. The transitions would be conducted by VMFAT-101 at El Toro.

The first A-6E unit at El Toro to be redesignated Marine All-Weather Fighter Attack Squadron (VMFA[AW]) was VMA(AW)-121,

emphasising the advent of a new role for the 'Green Knights', the fighter role. (Eventually, the squadron will also be tasked with the photo reconnaissance role.) Redesignation took place on 8 December 1989 and the first aircraft was received on 11 May 1990. The first training class of F/A-18D aircrews, consisting of six pilots and seven Weapons System Officers (WSO) started in February 1990. Barely eight months after receiving their first F/A-18D the 'Green Knights' were ordered to deploy to the Gulf region. One of the missions was replacing the vulnerable OV-10 Bronco (two Marine Corps OV-10s were lost early in the conflict to Iraqi groundfire) as Forward Air Control (FAC) aircraft and reinstituting the 'Fast FAC' concept employed during the war in SEA. The F/A-18D played a key part in the air and ground phases of the war in the Gulf, identifying fixed and moving enemy targets, day and night, directing other aircraft into position to attack the enemy targets. *McDonnell Douglas*

Left and Right:
F/A-18C (163505, AA-406) VFA-81, USS Saratoga
F/A-18C (163508, AA-401) VFA-81, USS Saratoga
Although during 'Desert Storm' USS *Saratoga's* CVW-17 flew the smallest number of combat missions (2,600+) of the six participating air wings (in comparison: *Ranger's* CVW-2 flew 4,200+ missions), it played a prominent role in ousting the Iraqis from Kuwait. The Wing's VFA-81 'Sunliners' shot down two Iraqi MiG-21 'Fishbeds' on 17 January 1991 — the Navy's first combat kills (initially it was announced that the Iraqi aircraft involved were MiG-29 'Fulcrums') validating the strike-fighter concept. The aircraft (163508/AA-401 flown by Lt-Cdr Mark Fox and 163502/AA-410 flown by Lt Nick Mongillo) were directed to their targets by an E-C2 Hawkeye (159107, AA-600) of *Sara's* VAW-125. When Fox and Mongillo received the bandits call they were part of a flight of four Hornets tasked with dropping four 2,000lb MK84 bombs each on an airfield in Western Iraq. After shooting down their MiG-21s with an AIM-9 Sidewinder (Fox) and AIM-7 Sparrow (Mongillo) the pilots switched back from the air-to-air to the air-to-ground mode and continued their mission.

However, VFA-81 also had the distinction of losing the Navy's first aircraft in combat. The F/A-18C (163484/AA-403) was hit by a SAM on 17 January. The pilot, Lt-Cdr Michael S. Speicher, was killed in action. (CVW-17 also lost one A-6E and an F-14B through enemy groundfire.) On 11 March, the USS *Saratoga* commenced redeployment to its homebase Mayport, Fl arriving on 28 March. The units of the air wing arrived one day earlier at NAS Oceana, Norfolk, *and* Cecil Field. During the deployment — 217 days at sea and 20 days in port CVW-17 flew 12,500 sorties totalling 33,000 flight hours. Squadrons flew 2,694 combat missions and delivered 4,047,000lb of ordnance on enemy targets.

VFA-81 was established on 1 July 1955 as an all weather fighter interceptor squadron flying the F9F-8 Cougar. Via the A-4 Skyhawk and A-7B Corsair, the 'Sunliners' converted to the 'E' version of the A-7 in February 1970, becoming the first East Coast recipient of the type. In the last three years of A-7E operation, the squadron won the ComNavAirLant Battle 'E'. After completing its 24th Mediterranean deployment (on board the USS *Forrestal*) VA-81 was redesignated VFA-81 on 4 February 1988 and started conversion to the F/A-18C. In early August 1990 VFA-81 deployed for the first time since 1987. *USAF by SRA Chris Putman/McDonnell Douglas*

Below:

F/A-18A (162826, XE-34) VX-5, NAS China Lake, Ca
Air Test and Evaluation Squadron (VX)-5 is a tenant at NAS China
Lake, Ca, operating out of Armitage Field. The squadron is part of
the Operational Test and Evaluation Force, Norfolk, Va. Its mission
is to conduct extensive tests of ordnance and aircraft equipment
and to develop and evaluate aircraft weapon tactics. Flight-testing
includes tests at all stages of weapon system development, as well
as final test and evaluation of air-to-ground weapons, rockets,
bombs, weapon components and control systems, flares and similar
devices. The 'Vampires' were commissioned on 18 June 1951 as Air
Development Squadron Five at NAS Moffett, Ca and were equipped
with nine AD-1 Skyraiders. In July 1956 the squadron was
redesignated Air Test and Evaluation Squadron and moved to China
Lake to take advantage of the outstanding weapon-delivery
facilities. In 1962 VX-5 became the first squadron to receive the
A-4E Skyhawk, while Detachment Alpha was assigned two A-6A
Intruders to evaluate the advanced weapon system. On
23 December 1967 delivery of the new A-7A Corsair II was made at
VX-5. Testing and evaluation included all available weapons and
nuclear configurations, and all manoeuvre tactics.

In 1981 the squadron aircraft inventory increased to 20 aircraft,
with an addition of several Hornets for the evaluation of the type.
January 1991 found VX-5 deployed to NAS Fallon, Nv with 14
airplanes and 300 personnel for two weeks. The purpose of the
squadron deployment was to develop F/A-18 LOT XII night
strike/fighter tactics, to ensure all aircrew were tactically proficient
and to exercise the mobility of the squadron. Strike packages were
flown in support of Operations 'Desert Shield' and 'Desert Storm'.
To carry out its mission VX-5 flies a variety of aircraft including the
A-6E, EA-6B, AH-1W and AV-8B. *US Navy by PH3 Robert C. Foster*

Above:

F/A-18A (161734, MF-00) VMFA-134, MCAS El Toro, Ca
Marine Corps Reserve flying units are organised within MAW-4,
with headquarters at NAS New Orleans, La. F-4 and A-4 squadrons
are continuing the transition process to the F/A-18 aircraft
currently being used by active forces. The first Marine Corps
Reserve unit to be equipped with the F/A-18 Hornet was VMFA-134
at MCAS El Toro, Ca conversion from the F-4S Phantom starting on
5 May 1989 with the arrival of the first Hornet. Full complement
was received by August 1989.

VMA-142, stationed at NAS Cecil Field, Fl became the second
unit to convert to F/A-18. The unit was redesignated VMFA-142 on
21 December 1990. VMFA-321, at NAF Andrews, Md (holding a
ceremony on 13 July 1991 to mark the retirement of their F-4S
aircraft) and VMFA-112, at NAS Dallas, Tx (F-4S) will transition to
the F/A-18 in FY92 and FY93 respectively.

MF-00, the squadron commander's aircraft, is pictured on
29 July 1989 on final approach to NAS Dallas, Tx. *Keith Snyder*

Left and Below:
F/A-18B (162870, SH-10) VMFAT-101, MCAS El Toro, Ca
F/A-18C (163713, SH-135) VMFAT-101, MCAS El Toro, Ca
When Marine Aircraft Group (MAG)-13 relocated on 1 October 1987 from MCAS El Toro, Ca, to MCAS Yuma, Az, Marine Combat Crew Readiness Training Group (MCCRTG)-10 had been disbanded one day earlier. The Group's Marine Fighter Attack Training Squadron (VMFAT)-101, flying the F-4S Phantom, was PCS-ed (Permanent Change of Station) to El Toro to become the Marine Corps F/A-18 Hornet Fleet Replacement Squadron while assigned to MAG-11. Until the move of VMFAT-101 to El Toro, Hornet PIlots were trained by VFA-125 at NAS Lemoore, Ca, and VFA-106 at NAS Cecil Field, Fl. The 'Sharpshooters' were commissioned at MCAS Yuma on 3 January 1969, and were temporarily attached to MAG-33 at MCAS El Toro. VMFAT-101 was awarded the Robert M. Hansen award in October 1983, presented to the most outstanding fighter squadron in Marine aviation. When the last US Navy F-4 training squadron was disbanded on 1 June 1984, VMFAT-101 took on responsibility for training pilots and RIOs of the US Navy, becoming the sole unit in the sea services actively training crews for the F-4 Phantom. VMFAT-101 operates all versions of the Hornet. It had accumulated 50,000 accident free flying hours over a five-year period in late 1990.

An F/A-18B and an F/A-18C of the 'Sharpshooters' are pictured on finals to NAS Dallas, Tx. After a short period of carrying two-digit numbers, the squadron resumed carrying three-digit numbers.
Both: Keith Snyder

capable rates exceeded 90%. The Hornets flew a total of more than 11,000 sorties, encompassing some 30,000 flight hours. 18,000,000lb of ordnance were dropped, involving 15 different types of weapons, including some 250 HARMs. 6000+ targets were attacked — including 24 main bases, 30 dispersal bases, command and control facilities and surface-to-surface missiles. The F/A-18s were 91.5% mission and 90.4% full mission capable. The aircraft of VFA-81 and 83 accumulated an average of 128.5 flight hours.

NAS Squantum, Ma was the official birthplace of VFA-83, originally Naval Reserve Fighter Squadron 916. Via NAS Oceana, the 'Rampagers' moved to NAS Cecil Field, Fl in 1966 and were the last to fly A-4s on board the USS *John F. Kennedy*. VA-83 transitioned to the A-7E, which was flown through 1987. On 1 March 1988, the 'Rampagers' became Strike Fighter Squadron 83, flying the 'C' model of the F/A-18 Hornet. *US Navy by CW02 Ed Bailey*

Right:
***F-18A (163099, AJ-406) VFA-87 USS* Theodore Roosevelt**
When 'Desert Storm' was initiated in the early hours of 17 January 1991, six aircraft carriers were present in the region: The USS *Ranger* and *Midway* in the Persian Gulf and the USS *America, Saratoga, John F. Kennedy* and *Theodore Roosevelt* in the Red Sea. The *Roosevelt* had left Norfolk on 28 December 1990 with CVW-8 embarked, arriving on station in the Red Sea on 14 January 1991. One week later the carrier moved in to the Persian Gulf region. During 'Desert Storm' aircraft of CVW-8 flew more than 4,200 sorties, dropping 4,500,000lb of ordnance on targets in Kuwait and Iraq. The squadron lost an F/A-18A on a combat mission on 5 February 1991, which was not attributed to hostile action. The pilot of the Hornet, Lt Robert J. Dwyer, was killed. After the cease-fire with Iraq, the USS *Theodore Roosevelt* moved to the Mediterranean and participated in Operation 'Provide Comfort'. Through air patrols and reconnaissance, aircraft of its air wing provided security to Kurdish refugees, fleeing from Iraqi forces. The carrier arrived home on 28 June 1991.

VFA-87 was officially established at NAS Cecil Field, Fl as Attack Squadron VA-87 on 1 February 1968 while attached to VA-174 and became fully operational in June 1968. The 'Golden Warriors' were the first East Coast squadron to fly the A-7B. Transition to the A-7E was commenced on 11 August 1975. After completing flight operations in the A-7E in March 1986, VA-87 became the first of the original fleet attack squadrons at NAS Cecil Field to convert to the F/A-18A Hornet. Redesignation to strike fighter squadron took place on 1 May 1986. VFA-87s first deployment was made aboard the USS *Theodore Roosevelt* as temporary member of CVW-1.
US Navy by PHC Denis Kesue

Above:
***F-18C (163509, AA-300) VFA-83 USS* Saratoga**
CVW-17s second strike fighter squadron on board the USS *Saratoga* during 'Desert Storm' was VFA-83, the 'Rampagers'. Although overshadowed by the successful downing of two Iraqi MiG-21 'Fishbeds' by VFA-83's sister squadron VFA-81, the 'Rampagers' participated significantly in the strike sorties flown by sea-service pilots against carefully planned targets — including anti-air defenses and ballistic missile launchers. On 30 January all 18 F/A-18Cs of CVW-17 delivered 100,000lb of MK83 1,000lb bombs on Iraqi positions in Kuwait, the largest amount of bomb tonnage carried in a single mission. There were more than 210 US Navy, Marine Corps and Canadian F/A-18s in 'Desert Storm'. Full-mission

Below:

F-18D (164224, DT-00) VMFA(AW)-242   El Toro, Ca

On 14 December 1990 VMA(AW)-242 at MCAS El Toro, Ca became the Marine Corps second squadron to convert from the A-6E Intruder to the F/A-18D Night Hornet and consequently received the new designation VMFA(AW)-242 (Marine All Weather Fighter Attack Squadron). In all 60 F/A-18Ds will replace a similar number of A-6Es in five VMA(AW) units, one squadron converting per year, while 12 F/A-18Ds will be received by VMFA(AW)-225 which was re-established on 1 July 1991. VMFA(AW)-242 was originally activated as Marine Torpedo Bombing Squadron 242 on 1 July 1943 at El Centro, Ca. After operations from inland bases on Espirtu Santo, Tinian, Iwo Jima and Guam VMTB-242 returned to the USA and was deactivated on 23 November 1945. On 1 October 1960 the squadron was reactivated as Marine Attack Squadron VMA-242 at MCAS Cherry Point, NC flying A-4 Skyhawks. Returning from a tour of duty at MCAS Iwakuni, Japan, the squadron was re-established at MCAS Cherry Point and redesignated VMA(AW)-242, becoming the first Marine Corps squadron to be equipped with the A-6A Intruder.

From 1 November 1966 to 8 September 1970 the 'Bats' flew 16,783 combat missions out of Da Nang Air Base, South Vietnam, delivering 85,990 tons of ordnance in North and South Vietnam and Laos. On 12 September 1970 VMA(AW)-242 arrived at MCAS El Toro to become the first A-6 equipped squadron in the Third Marine Aircraft Wing. In September 1977 the squadron transitioned to the A-6E and three-and-a-half years later VMA(AW)-242 started conversion to the A-6E (TRAM). In August 1983 the 'Bats' became the first Marine squadron to deploy to the African continent as part of Operation 'Eastern Wind 83' in Berbera, Somalia. VMA(AW)-242 frequently deployed to MCAS Iwakuni as part of the six-month Unit Deployment Program. On 21 December 1990 the squadron transferred its and El Toro's last A-6 Intruder to VA-52, while two months later (25 February 1991) their first F/A-18D was received.

Keith Snyder

Right:

F/A-18As of USMC enroute to Persian Gulf area

At the beginning of 'Desert Storm' more than 80% of the total Marine Corps air assets were deployed in South West Asia (SWA). Aircraft included AV-8B, EA-6B, KC-130T, OV-10B and F/A-18, helicopters included AH-1W, CH-46E and CH-53E. In total 241 fixed-wing and 325 rotary-wing aircraft were deployed, flying some 18,000 sorties. With its 241 aircraft the Marine Corps possessed 7% of the allied fixed-wing aircraft number, providing approximately 11% of the tactical fixed-wing sorties flown by all allied forces, and approximately 43% of those sorties flown by all US Naval air forces.

Included in the number of 241 Marine Corps fixed-wing aircraft were 84 F/A-18 Hornets: 12 F/A-18Ds, 36 F/A-18Cs and 36 F/A-18As. These aircraft flew a total of 5,047 'Desert Storm' sorties. The 84 F/A-18s were assigned to seven different squadrons: VMFA(AW)-121, VMFA-314 from MCAS El Toro, Ca respectively with F/A-18D and A; VMFA-333 and 451 from MCAS Beaufort, SC with F/A-18A and VMFA-212, 232 and 235 from MCAS Kaneohe Bay, HI with F/A-18C (leaving no Hornets there). The parent unit in the Gulf was MAG-11, which also included A-6E Intruders of VMA(AW)-224 and 533, EA-6B Prowlers of VMAQ-2 and KC-130F Hercules of VMGR-252, all from MCAS Cherry Point, NC, VMGR-352 from El Toro with KC-130F Hercules, and Det. VMGR-452 from Stewart AB, NY with130Ts, and was assigned to 3MAW. The Wing — provisional, as its flag was not moved, but stayed at El Toro — was the aviation combat element for the overall First Marine Expeditionary Force, 1 MEF. The deployment of Marine Corps F/A-18s was initiated on 20 August 1990, when VMFA-314 and 235 left their respective homestations. VMFA-333 and 451 left for the Gulf region one day later. Initially the squadrons were assigned to MAG-70 at Shaikh Isa, Bahrain. The Group was deactivated on 3 September when MAG-11 took over responsibility.

On 12 December VMFA-212 and 232 arrived at Shaikh Isa, one month later (14 January 1991) followed by the F/A-18Ds of VMFA(AW)-121. After the start of 'Desert Storm' the mission of the Hornets was expanded and included close air support, strike escort, battlefield air interdiction, offensive and defensive air-to-air missions and suppression of enemy air defenses. No combat sorties were missed due to maintenance problems. 95% of all sorties scheduled were completed. F/A-18As of VMFA-333 needed only 3.73 maintenance manhours per flight hour, while flying 884.7 hours.

The Marine Corps suffered no F/A-18 combat losses, but lost two aircraft in non-combat operations. On 9 March two F/A-18Cs collided in mid-air over Saudi Arabia. Both pilots ejected and landed safely by parachute. Three Hornets were damaged by SAMs and

one by AAA, but they returned safely and the aircraft were back in service within 48 hours. (One of the aircraft was hit in both engines and flew 125 miles to its homebase for recovery.)

Redeployment was initiated on 24 March with the return home of VMFA-314, followed by VMFA-333 and 451 (1 April), VMFA-232 and 235 (2 April) and finally VMFA-212 and VMFA(AW)-121 (15 May).

USAF by SSgt Scott Stewart

Below:

F/A-18A(R) (161214) McDonnell Douglas, St Louis, Mo
An F/A-18 Hornet with reconnaissance equipment made the first flight from St Louis, Mo, on 15 August 1984. During the 1hr flight, the handling qualities and performance of the recce equipment were tested. To allow the aircraft to accomplish the mission, the 20mm M61A1 gun and ammo-drum were temporarily removed and replaced by a reconnaissance equipment pallet. Return to a full fighter/attack capability was expected to take place in less than eight hours. Originally, the recce installation was tested aboard the first Hornet built, 160775.

After approval of the recce provisions in May 1987, the Systems Engineering Test Directorate at NATC, NAS Patuxent River, Md, developed a recce version of the Hornet designated the F/A-18(R). It is the second production F/A-18, c/n 161214. Testing was carried out at NAS Patuxent River, and was designed merely to determine whether the F/A-18 would be a suitable platform for a

reconnaissance mission. A recce-capable F/A-18D (D1, 163434) suited to carry the Control Data Corporation ATARS (Advanced Tactical Reconnaissance System) is to start flight testing at NAS Patuxent River, Md in January 1992. The ATARS is a digital sensor suite and comprises of low and medium altitude electro-optical sensors, an infrared sensor, tape recorders and data link. The ATARS will be installed in place of the nose gun. The Marine Corps Acquisition Objective is 31, although this number was later increased to 48. Of the first 31 ATARS the last two are expected to be funded in FY95. IOC is scheduled for FY94. *McDonnell Douglas*

Right:

F-18A (160778, 4) McDonnell Douglas, St Louis, Mo
When this photograph was taken in March 1980 of the No 4 pre-production aircraft (160778) flying over the river front in St Louis, Mo, McDonnell Douglas still talked about the development of the F-18 in two versions. The fighter escort to replace the F-4, and the light attack aircraft to replace the A-7.

As of 22 April 1991 1,000 Hornets have been delivered to the US Marine Corps, US Navy, Canada, Australia and Spain, accumulating more than 1.2 million flight hours. The number 1,000 was the 72nd F/A-18D (164237), part of Block 33 and one of 84 Hornets the Navy ordered in FY89. It was assigned to VMFA(AW)-242 at MCAS El Toro, Ca (as DT-03), the second Marine Corps A-6E unit to convert to the F/A-18D. The mission capable rate for the F/A-18 is above 80%. The July 1989-June 1990 maintenance manhours per flight hour (maintainability) was 25.5 for F/A-18 operational USMC/USN squadrons compared to 44.8 for the A-7E and 62.4 for the F-14A. The July 1989-June 1990 mean flight hours between failure (reliability) as 2.0 for the F/A-18, 0.9 for the A-7E and 0.5 for the F-14A. The F/A-18 USMC/USN loss rate as of 1 August 1990 was 4.7/100,000 flight hours (of which 1.4 were aircraft-related). A total of 22 USMC/USN Hornets were lost in the first USMC/USN) 500,000 flight hours. (In comparison: 111 A7s and 95 F-4s were lost.) The loss rate dropped to 4.52 based on 796,000 flying hours and 36 losses. Ease of maintenance is one of the other advantages of the Hornet. The ability to do one complete engine change in as little as two hours on the F/A-18, and have the aircraft on the catapult, compares with at least six hours needed for the A-7E.

The Marine Corps is continuing to develop and refine the expeditionary qualities of the Hornet. Concept development is underway to conduct F/A-18 operations from FOBs (Forward Operating Bases) in much the same manner as the AV-8B. When married up with new, portable arresting gear, the Hornet will be capable of operating from expeditionary surfaces less than 2,000ft long.

APPENDIX

Unit	Code	Name	Type	Replacing/Converted from
US MARINE CORPS				
MCAS Beaufort, SC		MAW-2/MAG-31		
VMFA-115	VE	Silver Eagles	F/A-18A	F-4S
VMFA-122	DC	Crusaders	F/A-18A	F-4S
VMFA-251	DW	Thunderbolts	F/A-18A	F-4S
VMFA-312	DR	Checkertails	F/A-18CN	F/A-18A
VMFA-333	DN	Shamrocks	F/A-18A	F-4S
VMFA-451	VM	Warlords	F/A-18A	F-4S
MCAS El Toro, Ca		MAW-3/MAG-11		
VMFA-314	VW	Black Knights	F/A-18A	F-4N
VMFA-323	WS	Death Rattlers	F/A-18A	F-4N
VMFA-531	EC	Grey Ghosts	F/A-18A	F-4N
VMFA(AW)-121	VK	Green Knights	F/A-18D	A-6E
VMFA(AW)-242	DT	Bats	F/A-18D	A-6E
VMFA(AW)-225	CE	Vikings	F/A-18D	–
VMFAT-101	SH	Sharpshooters	F/A-18A/B/C/D	F-4S
MCAS Kaneohe Bay, Hi		MAB-1/MAG-24		
VMFA-212	WD	Lancers	F/A-18C	F-4S
VMFA-232	WT	Red Devils	F/A-18C	F-4S
VMFA-235	DB	Death Angels	F/A-18C	F-4S
US MARINE CORPS/RESERVE				
MCAS El Toro, Ca		MAW-4/MAG-46		
VMFA-134	MF	Hawks	F/A-18A	F-4S
NAS Cecil Field, Fl		MAW-4/MAG-42, Det A		
VMFA-142	MB	Flying Gators	F/A-18A	A-4M
NAF Washington DC		MAW-4/MAG-41, Det A		
VMFA-321	MG	Black Barons	F/A-18A	F-4S
US NAVY				
NAF Atsugi, Japan				
VFA-192	NF	Golden Dragons	F/A-18C	F/A-18A
VFA-195	NF	Dam Busters	F/A-18C	F/A-18A
NAS Cecil Field, Fl				
VFA-15	AJ	Valions	F/A-18A	A-7E
VFA-37	AC	Bulls	F/A-18CN	A-7E
VFA-81	AA	Sunliners	F/A-18C	A-7E
VFA-82	AB	Marauders	F/A-18C	A-7E
VFA-83	AA	Rampagers	F/A-18C	A-7E
VFA-86	AB	Sidewinders	F/A-18C	A-7E
VFA-87	AJ	Golden Warriors	F/A-18A	A-7E
VFA-105	AC	Gunslingers	F/A-18CN	A-7E
VFA-106	AD	Gladiators	F/A-18A/B/C/D	–
VFA-131	AG	Wildcats	F/A-18CN	F/A-18A
VFA-132	AE	Privateers	F/A-18A	–
VFA-136	AG	Knight Hawks	F/A-18CN	F/A-18A
VFA-137	AE	Kestrels	F/A-18A	–
NAS Lemoore, Ca				
VFA-22	NH	Fighting Redcocks	F/A-18CN	A-7E
VFA-25	NK	Fist of the Fleet	F/A-18CN	F/A-18A
VFA-27	NL	Chargers	F/A-18A	A-7E
VFA-94	NH	Shrikes	F/A-18CN	A-7E
VFA-97	NL	Warhawks	F/A-18A	A-7E
VFA-113	NK	Stingers	F/A-18CN	F/A-18A
VFA-125	NJ	Rough Raiders	F/A-18A/B/C/D	–
VFA-146	NG	Blue Diamonds	F/A-18C	A-7E
VFA-147	NG	Argonauts	F/A-18CN	A-7E
VFA-151	NM	Vigilantes	F/A-18A	F-4S
VFA-161	NM	Chargers	F/A-18A	F-4S
US NAVY/RESERVE				
VFA-203	AF	Blue Dolphins	F/A-18A	A-7E
VFA-204	AF	River Rattlers	F/A-18A	A-7E
VFA-303	ND	Golden Hawks	F/A-18A	A-7B
VFA-305	ND	Lobos	F/A-18A	A-7B
MISC UNITS				
VX-4	XF	Evaluators	F/A-18A, C, D	
VX-5	XE	Vampires	F/A-18A, C, D	
VAQ-34	–	Flashbacks	F/A-18A, B	
NATC*/SATD	SD	–	F/A-18A, C, D	
NSWC	–	Strike University	F/A-18A, B	
NWC*	–	–	F/A-18A, C, D	
NWEF*	–	–	F/A-18A	

Unit	Code	Name	Type	Replacing/Converted from
PMTC*	—	—	F/A-18A, B, C	
TPS	—	—	F/A-18B	
USNFDT	—	Blue Angels	F/A-18A, B	
NASA	—	—	F/A-18A, B	
MACAIR	—	—	F/A-18	

CVW	Carrier	Remarks
CVW-5	USS Independence	USS Midway
CVW-5	USS Independence	USS Midway
CVW-5	USS Theodore Roosevelt	
CVW-3	USS John F. Kennedy	
CVW-17	USS Saratoga	
CVW-1	USS America	
CVW-17	USS Saratoga	
CVW-1	USS America	
CVW-8	USS Theodore Roosevelt	
CVW-3	USS John F. Kennedy	
—	—	East Coast FRS
CVW-7	USS Dwight D. Eisenhower	
CVW-6	USS Forrestal	To be disest. Spring 1992
CVW-7	USS Dwight D. Eisenhower	
CVW-6	USS Forrestal	To CVW-2/USS Constellation
CVW-11	USS Abraham Lincoln	
CVW-14	USS Carl Vinson	From USS Midway
CVW-15	USS Kitty Hawk	
CVW-11	USS Abraham Lincoln	
CVW-15	USS Kitty Hawk	
CVW-14	USS Carl Vinson	From USS Midway
—	—	West Coast FRS
CVW-9	USS Nimitz	
CVW-9	USS Nimitz	
—	—	NAS Lamoore, Ca; to CVW-2 1992/USS Constellation
CVW-10	(USS Independence)	Disest. 1 April 1988
CVWR-20	—	NAS Cecil Field, Fl
CVWR-20	—	NAS New Orleans, La
CVWR-30	—	NAS Lemoore, Ca
CVWR-30	—	NAS Point Mugu, Ca
—	—	NAS Lamoore, Ca; to CVW-2 1992/USS Constellation

NAS Point Mugu, Ca
NAS China Lake, Ca
NAS Lemoore, Ca: From NAS Point Mugu May 1991; 1st F/A-18 Jan 1992
NAS Patuxent River, Md: Naval Air Test Center/Strike Aircraft Test Directorate
NAS Fallon, NV: Naval Strike Warfare Center
NAS China Lake, Ca: Naval Weapons Center
Kirtland AFB, NM: Naval Weapons Evaluation Facility
NAS Point Mugu, Ca: Pacific Missile Test Center
NAS Patuxent River, Md: Test Pilot School
NAS Pensacola, Fl: US Navy Flight Demonstration Team
Edwards AFB, Ca: National Aeronautics & Space Administration
St Louis, Mo: McDonnell Aircraft Company

*Disestablished 1 January 1992 and consolidated within Naval Air Warfare Center (NAWC).

HORNETS ASSIGNED TO THE FSD PROGRAM

F1	160775		Flying qualities and flutter characteristics\
F2	160776		Performance and propulsion
F3	160777		Carrier trails
F4	160778		Envelope expansion and development
F5	160779		Weapons system development
F6	160780		High angle-of-attack development
T1	160781		Weapons system development
F7	160782		Weapons system development
F8	160783		Weapons system development
T2	160784		Aircraft availability and ease of maintainability
F9	160785		Aircraft availability and ease of maintainability

PROCUREMENT PROGRAM (USCM/USN)

Fiscal Year	Type	No. of aircraft	Serial number	Remarks
FY79	A/B	9	161213-217 161248-251	B: 217 B: 249
FY80	A/B	25	161353-367 161519-528	B: 354/57, 60
FY81	A/B	60	161702/761	B: 704, 07, 11, 14, 19, 23, 27, 33, 40, 46
FY82	A/B	64	161924-987	B: 924, 32, 38, 43, 47
FY83	A/B	84	162394-477	B: 402, 08, 13, 19, 27
FY84	A/B	84	162826-909	B: 836, 42, 50, 57, 64, 70, 76, 85
FY85	A/B	84	163092-175	B: 104, 10, 15, 23
FY86	C/D	84	163427/510	D: 434, 36, 41, 45, 47, 52, 54, 57, 60, 64, 68, 72, 74, 79, 82, 86, 88, 92, 97, 500, 01, 07,10
FY87	C/D	84	163699-782	D: 700, 07, 20, 34, 49, 63, 71, 78
FY88	C/D	84	163985-4068	D: 986, 89, 91, 94, 97, 001, 05, 09,11, 11, 14, 17, 19, 22, 24, 26, 28, 32, 35, 38, 40, 43, 46, 49, 51, 53, 56, 58, 61, 64, 68
FY89	C/D	84	164196-279	D: 196, 98, 203, 07, 11, 16, 19, 24, 28, 33, 37, 41, 45, 49, 54, 59, 63, 67, 72, 79
FY90	C/D	66	164627-692	D: 649/53, 56, 59, 62, 65, 67, 70, 72, 74, 77, 79, 83, 85, 88, 90, 92
FY91	C/D	48	164693-740	D: 694, 99, 702, 05, 11, 14, 17, 23, 26, 29, 35, 38
FY92	C/D	48	164865-912	D: 866, 69, 73, 76, 80, 83, 86, 89, 93, 97, 901, 04, 07, 10
FY93	C/D	48		
FY94	C/D	54		
FY95	C/D	54		
FY96	C/D	54		

PROCUREMENT PROGRAM (CANADA)   FY81/FY86

CF-18A   188701-798 (98)
CF-18B   188901-940 (40)

PROCUREMENT PROGRAM (AUSTRALIA)   FY83/FY87

F/A-18A   A21-1/57 (57)
F/A-18B   A21-101/118 (18)

PROCUREMENT PROGRAM (SPAIN)   FY84/FY88

EF-18A   C.15-13/72 (60)
EF-18B   CE.15-1/12 (12)

PROCUREMENT PROGRAM (KUWAIT)   FY90/FY91

F/A-18C   401-432 (32)
F/A-18D   441-448 (8)

AUSTRALIA
(all units fly both F/A-18A and F/A-18B aircraft)

3 Squadron*		Williamtown, NSW	Mirage III O
75 Squadron		Tindal, NT	Mirage III O/OD
77 Squadron*	Magpie	Williamtown, NSW	Mirage IIi O/OD
2 OCU*	Tiger	Williamtown, NSW	Mirage III O/OD

*Assigned to No 81 Fighter Wing

CANADA
(all units fly both CF-18A and CF-18B aircraft)

409 Squadron (TF)*	Nighthawk	Baden-Söllingen, FRG	CF-101B/F
410 Squadron (TFT)	Cougar	Cold Lake, Alberta	CF-101B/F
416 Squadron (TF)	Lynx	Cold Lake, Alberta	CF-101B/F
421 Squadron (TF)**	Red Indian	Baden-Söllingen, FRG	CF-104D/G
425 Squadron (TF)	Alouette	Bagotville, Quebec	CF-101B/F
433 Squadron (TF)	Porcupine	Bagotville, Quebec	CF-5A/D
439 Squadron (TF)**	Tiger	Baden-Söllingen, FRG	CF-104D/G
441 Squadron (TF)	Silver Fox	Cold Lake, Alberta	CF-104D/G
Aircraft Engineering Test Establishment (AETE)		Cold Lake, Alberta	–

*Disbanded 25 June 1991
**Assigned to No 4 Fighter Wing; to return to Canada by 1994

SPAIN
(all units fly both EF-18A and EF-18B aircraft)

121 Squadron*	Poker	Torrejon	F-4C
122 Squadron*	Tenis	Torrejon	F-4C
151 Squadron**	Ebro	Zaragoza	–
152 Squadron**	Marte	Zaragoza	–

*Assigned to Ala de Caza 12
**Assigned to Ala de Caza 15